THE DAUGHTERS OF GEORGE III

SISTERS AND PRINCESSES

To Anne – a princess in every sense of the word!

THE DAUGHTERS OF GEORGE III

SISTERS AND PRINCESSES

CATHERINE CURZON

PEN & SWORD HISTORY

AN IMPRINT OF PEN & SWORD BOOKS LTD.
YORKSHIRE – PHILADELPHIA

First published in Great Britain in 2020 by
PEN AND SWORD HISTORY
An imprint of
Pen & Sword Books Ltd
Yorkshire – Philadelphia

ISBN 978 1 47389 753 3

Printed and bound in the UK by TJ International
Typeset in Times New Roman 11.5/14 by
Aura Technology and Software Services, India.

Pen & Sword Books Limited incorporates the imprints of Atlas, Archaeology,
Aviation, Discovery, Family History, Fiction, History, Maritime, Military, Military
Classics, Politics, Select, Transport, True Crime, Air World, Frontline Publishing,
Leo Cooper, Remember When, Seaforth Publishing, The Praetorian Press,
Wharncliffe Local History, Wharncliffe Transport, Wharncliffe True Crime and
White Owl.

For a complete list of Pen & Sword titles please contact
PEN & SWORD BOOKS LIMITED
47 Church Street, Barnsley, South Yorkshire, S70 2AS, England
E-mail: enquiries@pen-and-sword.co.uk
Website: www.pen-and-sword.co.uk

Or
PEN AND SWORD BOOKS
1950 Lawrence Rd, Havertown, PA 19083, USA
E-mail: Uspen-and-sword@casematepublishers.com
Website: www.penandswordbooks.com

Contents

Contents

Illustrations

Illustrations

24. Frances Burney by Charles Turner, 1840.
25. The Apotheosis of Princes Octavius and Alfred by Sir Robert Strange, after Benjamin West, 1787.
26. HRH Princess Elizabeth.
27. HRH Princess Mary.
28. The royal family of England in the year 1787 by Thomas Stothard, 1800.
29. Royal Beneficence by Charles Howard Hodges, after Thomas Stothard, 1793.
30. The Hombourg Waltz, showing Elizabeth and the Prince of Hesse-Homburg by G Humphrey.
31. Caricature of the Introduction of the Duke of Württemberg (afterwards King Frederick I) to George III and Queen Charlotte previous to his marriage with Charlotte, Princess Royal of England, by Anthony Pasquin.
32. Lady Charlotte Finch by John Faber the Younger, after John Robinson.

Plates 1, 2, 3, 4, 5, 6, 9, 12, 15, 19, 21, 22, 26, 27: Courtesy of Internet Archive Book Images. Public domain.

Plates 7, 16, 29: Courtesy of Rijksmuseum, under Creative Commons Public Domain Dedication CC0 1.0 Universal licence. http:// creativecommons. org/publicdomain/zero/1.0/deed.en

Plates 8, 10, 14, 17, 18, 25: Courtesy Wellcome Library, London, under Creative Commons Attribution only licence CC BY 4.0 http:// creativecommons.org/licenses/by/4.0/

Plate 11: Courtesy of the University of Michigan. Public domain.

Plates 13, 20, 31, 32: Courtesy of The Yale Center for British Art. Public domain.

Plates 23, 24: From The New York Public Library Public domain.

Plates 28, 30: From the British Cartoon Prints Collection (Library of Congress). No known restrictions on publication.

Acknowledgements

I've spent a long, long time in the company of the six daughters of George and Charlotte, and my first thank you is to those remarkable women. It's been a true pleasure getting to know them.

As ever, the tireless and indefatigable team at Pen & Sword are worthy of nothing but praise. A particularly big piece of cake should go to Jon and the *still* fierce and fabulous Lucy, editor extraordinaire!

I'm also sending out thanks across the world for everyone who has ever read anything I've written or taken the time to tell me to keep on keeping on. To Adrian, Rob, and Debra, a shower of hugs and thanks just for being you. And of course, UTT.

I send bubbles and biscuits to Pippa, Nelly, and the Rakish Colonial – the prince and princesses in *my* life.

Introduction

'Poor old wretches as we are [...] a dead weight upon you, old lumber to the country, like old clothes, I wonder you do not vote for putting us in a sack and drowning us in the Thames.'[1]

When Princess Sophia of the United Kingdom put pen to paper in 1811 to write to her brother, the Prince Regent, she was still a woman in her mid-thirties. Yet as far as she was concerned, her life was over. She believed that she was condemned to remain forever at home, nothing more than companion to a resentful mother and a comfort to a fading father. At Sophia's side were three of her five sisters, each preserved as if in aspic at Windsor. Only one of the princesses had escaped what became known as *the nunnery*, marrying into European royalty and queening it over her own court. The youngest of the six sisters was already dead.

These were the daughters of King George III and his bride, Charlotte of Mecklenburg-Strelitz.

The princesses were born into that most unusual royal marriage – a faithful one. Though blighted by the mental illness that eventually saw his eldest son appointed as Prince Regent, George III broke with the tradition of his predecessors by eschewing mistresses and sexual intrigue. Instead he remained loyal to his wife for almost sixty years. To the Georgian public, George and Charlotte were the model of respectability. The same could not be said for all of their offspring, however.

Their sons were a handful, to put it mildly. Their daughters didn't really get the chance to misbehave, but that didn't stop them from becoming fascinating women, and the six daughters of George III each have their own story to tell. From accomplished childhood to isolated adulthood, not to mention crowns, lovers and even rumours of illegitimate children, life as a Georgian princess veered wildly from excitement to boredom, with the odd foray into the downright bizarre.

With six princesses to bring back to life and only a finite number of words in which to do so, we shall start our tale with their shared childhood, before joining each princess as she makes her way into the world. For some, the future was one of husbands, courts and travel whilst for others it was seclusion, frustration and maybe a quiet little scandal now and then.

It has been my pleasure to spend time with these six women and I hope you'll enjoy getting to know these very different princesses who were moulded in one of the most insular courts of the long eighteenth century.

These are the women of the Windsor nunnery, sisters and princesses.

Meet the Children

King George III and Charlotte of Mecklenburg-Strelitz had fifteen children, all born in the first twenty-two years of their marriage. Remarkably, all of them survived their births – no small achievement in the eighteenth century. Their names are below, and where appropriate, their legal spouses are italicised beneath. Illegitimate marriages (George IV, you know who you are!) aren't included, for the sake of simplicity.

George IV (12 August 1762 - 26 June 1830)
Princess Caroline of Brunswick-Wolfenbüttel
Prince Frederick, Duke of York and Albany (16 August 1763 - 5 January 1827)
Princess Frederica of Prussia
William IV (21 August 1765 - 20 June 1837)
Princess Adelaide of Saxe-Meiningen
Charlotte, Princess Royal (29 September 1766 - 6 October 1828)
King Frederick of Württemberg
Prince Edward, Duke of Kent and Strathearn (2 November 1767 - 23 January 1820)
Princess Victoria of Saxe-Coburg-Saalfeld
Princess Augusta Sophia (8 November 1768 - 22 September 1840)
Princess Elizabeth (22 May 1770 - 10 January 1840)
Frederick, Landgrave of Hesse-Homburg
Ernest Augustus, King of Hanover (5 June 1771 - 18 November 1851)
Princess Friederike of Mecklenburg-Strelitz
Prince Augustus Frederick, Duke of Sussex (27 January 1773 - 21 April 1843)
Lady Cecilia Buggin
Prince Adolphus, Duke of Cambridge (24 February 1774 - 8 July 1850)
Princess Augusta of Hesse-Kassel

Princess Mary, Duchess of Gloucester and Edinburgh (25 April 1776 -
30 April 1857)
Prince William Frederick, Duke of Gloucester and Edinburgh
Princess Sophia (3 November 1777 - 27 May 1848)
Prince Octavius (23 February 1779 - 3 May 1783)
Prince Alfred (22 September 1780 - 20 August 1782)
Princess Amelia (7 August 1783 - 2 November 1810)

Act One

A King, A Queen, and a Family of Fifteen

'A little after Twelve o'Clock on Tuesday, her Majesty [Charlotte of Mecklenburg-Strelitz] came to Rumford, where she [...] entered the King's Coach. The Attendants of her Majesty were in three other Coaches: In the first there were some Ladies from Mecklenburg, and in the last was her Majesty, who sat forward, and the Duchesses of Ancaster and Hamilton backward. Her Majesty was dressed entirely in the English Taste; she wore a Fly-Cap, with rich laced Lappets, a Stomacher ornamented with Diamonds, and a Gold Brocade Suit of Cloaths [sic], with a White Ground. They proceeded [to] the Garden-gate of the Palace; where her Majesty was handed out of her Coach by the Duke of Devonshire, as Lord-Chamberlain, to the Gate, where she was received by his Royal Highness the Duke of York. As her Majesty alighted from her Coach, his Majesty descended the Steps from the Palace into the Garden, and they met each other half-way; and as her Majesty was going to pay her Obediance, the King took hold of her Hand, raised her up, saluted it, and then led her up Stairs.

[...]

All the Royal Family, together with his Royal Highness the Duke of Cumberland, and Princess Amelia, were present at the Nuptials. Their Majesties, after the Ceremony, sat on one side of the Altar, on two State Chairs under a canopy; her Royal Highness the Princess Dowager of Wales sat facing them, in a Chair

1

of State, on the other Side; and all the rest of the Royal Family on Stools.

[...]

The Marriage Ceremony began at Nine at Night; at the Conclusion of which, the Guns at the Park and the Tower were fired, and the Cities of London and Westminster, &c, finely illuminated. The Rejoycings were universally expressed by the People, with that Chearfulness which true Loyalty inspires on this happy Occasion.'[1]

On 8 September 1761, 17-year-old Charlotte of Mecklenburg-Strelitz married King George III of the United Kingdom. She was six years his junior and until that day, the couple had never met. George had been on the throne just short of a year[2] and he was lacking a bride to get on with the business of creating heirs, which meant that a quick, respectable, Protestant marriage was vital. George was looking for a wife who was devout, free from scandal and with no political ambition. There had been potential candidates in George's youth, but none were suitable for the role of Queen Consort. Instead Parliament took it upon itself to do a little matchmaking and assembled a list of likely brides for the young sovereign's attention.

After much discussion, the longlist was whittled down into a manageable shortlist and given to the bachelor monarch. He looked through it and declared that nobody on the list appealed to him. Back to the politicians it went, and they put their heads together again and drew up a second selection for the Sovereign's consideration. This time George ran his critical eye down the names and added some of his own for good measure. He wrote to the future prime minister and his childhood mentor, Lord Bute, to say that, 'Our evening has been spent looking in the New Berlin Almanack for Princesses, where three new ones have been found, as yet unthought of.'[3] Among those three names was that of Princess Sophia Charlotte of Mecklenburg-Strelitz, the woman who was to become his bride.

'She is not tall, nor a beauty; pale, and very thin; but looks sensible, and is genteel. Her hair is darkish and fine; her forehead low, her nose very well, except the nostrils spreading too wide; her mouth has the same fault, but her teeth are good. She talks a good deal and French tolerably.'[4]

Charlotte was the perfect candidate. Her short life had been entirely untouched by scandal or controversy and after some time to consider, George took up his pen and wrote that Charlotte was his choice. 'I am resolv'd to fix it here,' he decided, though, ''tis not in every particular as I could wish.'[5] In other words, she'd have to do.

But as innumerable other royals would have been able to tell him, in matters of dynastic eighteenth century marriages, to have 'every particular' as one could wish for was rare indeed. As Charlotte and George stood before the Archbishop of Canterbury, Thomas Secker, in the Chapel Royal of St James's Palace, little did they know that they were about to embark on one of the most successful royal marriages in the history of the British throne.

Charlotte and George were to eventually become parents to fifteen children. Though not all would reach adulthood, to endure so many births and to encounter no losses in infancy was a feat in itself. The royal children were raised in a home that was loving, regimented, and regal and it's necessary to see what that upbringing involved if we are to understand the women it created. So, before we follow our princesses into their individual adulthoods, let's visit their shared nursery.

The First Daughter

'THIS morning, between eight and nine o'clock, the Queen was happily delivered of a Princess. Her Royal Highness the Princess Dowager of Wales, his Grace the Archbishop of Canterbury, and several Lords of his Majesty's most honourable Privy Council, and the Ladies of his Majesty's Bedchamber, were present.

Her Majesty is, God be praised, as well as can be expected; and the young Princess is in perfect health.

This great event was immediately made known by the firing of the Tower guns; and in the evening there were bonfires, illuminations, and other demonstrations of joy, in London and Westminster.'[6]

In the eighteenth century, much as today – though you won't find anybody admitting it – the heir and the spare was a concept that was very close to royal hearts. The family from Hanover had first settled its rump on the British throne in 1714, when George I left his beloved German electorate and became the very first Georgian king of Great Britain. He was succeeded by his son, George II, and in 1760 it was the turn of George III, the grandson of his predecessor. He was just 22 when he came to the throne and after his grumpy German namesakes, he was determined to be a breath of fresh British air.

George and Charlotte were devoted to one another and they didn't waste a moment when it came to producing heirs. Just ten months after their marriage Charlotte gave birth to George, the Prince of Wales. He was the heir to the throne who was later to become infamous as *Prinny*, the decadent Prince Regent. Almost exactly one year later, the spare, Frederick, Duke of York and Albany, came along and two years after *that* the family welcomed William, who would eventually reign as King William IV.

With three sons safely delivered and as healthy as any parents could wish for, Charlotte and George were ready for a change. To be more precise, they were ready for a little girl. They were about to get their wish.

During her three previous pregnancies Charlotte had been attended by her midwife, Mrs Draper, but for this pregnancy her usual retainer wasn't present. Although the esteemed royal physician and anatomist, Dr William Hunter, had previously been present when the queen delivered her children, he had never played a hands-on role. This time, however, he was to lead the proceedings. Lady Mary Coke, a noblewoman who provided waspish commentary on all aspects of court life, commented that the absence of Mrs Draper and the promotion of Hunter was 'kept as great a secret as if the fate of the country depended on this change'[7]. Lady Mary was desperate to know what had happened but Hunter, of course, was telling nobody anything.

On the morning of 29 September 1766, Princess Charlotte Augusta Matilda was born, and each of her names carried the weight one might expect of a royal family. Charlotte, of course, was the name of her mother. Augusta was the name of her paternal grandmother whilst Matilda was a name chosen in honour of the king's sister, Caroline Matilda. At the time of Charlotte's birth, that other young princess was packed and ready to leave England for Denmark, where she would begin a scandalous and controversial new life as the queen of King Christian VII, and the lover of his doctor, Johann Friedrich Struensee, but that is a tale for another time.[8]

In addition to her many names, the firstborn princess was also given the title of *Princess Royal*, which was traditionally awarded to the eldest daughter of the monarch. Charlotte was only the fourth of such princesses and at the time of writing, there have been just seven in total[9]. She knew that she was among a select group and as the years passed, she was determined to do justice to such an exclusive title, becoming known to all and sundry (including us) simply as *Royal*. After all, 'there has not been a Princess Royal born, while her Father was King of England, since the Reign of King Charles I, whose eldest Daughter, Princess Mary, was Mother of our glorious Deliverer King William III.'[10]

As the infant Royal settled in her cradle, the great and good flocked to Carlton House to pay their respects. They were received there by George's mother, Augusta of Saxe-Gotha, the Dowager Princess of Wales. She was also the baby Princess Royal's only surviving grandparent. Augusta had been widowed by the death of George's father, Frederick, Prince of Wales, fifteen years earlier and Charlotte's parents were also both deceased[11], which meant that the Dowager Princess could expect to be very busy with well-wishers for the foreseeable future.

Awash with excitement, the most illustrious names in the land flocked to St James's Palace where George III received their glad tidings. It wasn't only the wealthy who wanted to celebrate. In keeping with tradition, a thanksgiving event was held at the palace so that those who wished to pay their respects could visit St James's and receive a gift of caudle – a sweet, hot drink rather like eggnog - and cake. Unfortunately, the royal household had vastly underestimated the public excitement over the birth of the new princess and by the time the doors were due to be opened at 5.00 pm, there was a crowd of thousands waiting outside.

As word went around that the doors were being opened, the crowd surged forward and those at the front of the queue were crushed. Seeing that lives were at risk, the palace guards allowed a few people who were in danger of physical injury into the palace, but the excitement swelled to such proportions that they had to draw their weapons to hold back the unruly and panicked crowd. To avoid a disaster, the doors were closed and bolted with most well-wishers left outside. They went home disappointed, with their hopes of a celebration soured thanks to the crowd control, or lack of it.

The care of the Princess Royal was entrusted to a nurse named Mrs Chapman, who had also cared for the princess' brothers. Alongside her was a crack team including the royal governess, Lady Charlotte Finch, and a wet nurse named Frances Muttlebury. This most intimate of roles is one that raises modern eyebrows but in the Georgian era, for the queen *not* to have employed a wet nurse would have raised plenty of eyebrows too. Mrs Muttlebury was well paid in cash and gifts for her services and when she joined the family at Royal's christening on 27 October, she was dressed in a white satin and lace gown that the queen had provided. When one's attending a baptism by the Archbishop of Canterbury, one must keep up appearances.

For the wet nurse, caring for Royal was a time-consuming but richly rewarding role. On the cutting of Royal's first tooth, her nurse was given her choice of either a silver urn or £200 in cash. She went for the urn.

Smart woman.

Filling the Nursery

'Tuesday, about Seven o'Clock in the Evening, her Majesty was taken in Labour, of which Notice was immediately sent to her Royal Highness the Princess Dowager of Wales, his Grace the Archbishop of Canterbury, the two Secretaries of State, and Ladies of the Bed-Chamber, &c. who attended; when, at Half an Hour past Eight, her Majesty was safely delivered of a Princess. Her Majesty and the Princess were Yesterday as well as could be expected.'[12]

Royal was still a babe in arms when her first sister was born. As the queen's latest pregnancy progressed both George and Charlotte longed for a second daughter to be a friend to Royal and perhaps to balance out the male-dominated nursery. Perhaps displaying a hint of the anxiety and the obsessive tendencies that would later plague him, George became distracted by his thoughts of the gender of the new baby. Nothing but a little girl would do.

As Charlotte approached her due date and the king obsessed over the gender of the infant, Dr Hunter suggested that another little boy wouldn't be the end of the world. After all, he noted, 'whoever sees those lovely

Princes above stairs must be glad to have another.' Yet the single-minded monarch wasn't about to be placated and shot back that, 'Whoever sees that lovely child the Princess Royal above stairs must wish to have a fellow to her.'[13]

Happily, for Dr Hunter, the king got his wish on the evening of 8 November 1768 when Princess Augusta Sophia made her first appearance at the Queen's House. Augusta was named after her paternal grandmother. The new princess was passed into the arms of her nurse, Mrs Dorothy Thursby, and the family gathered to celebrate the happy event. Bells rang and guns fired and across the land, the news was proclaimed.

Thankfully this time, there were no crushes among the well-wishers. Once again, the public gathered at St James's for their caudle and once again, things got a little out of hand. Two enterprising and greedy young ladies were spotted by guards making off not only with more than their fair share of cake, but even a few of the pricy caudle cups. It was a sorry show that threatened to sour the celebratory atmosphere but once caught, the women were mortified. They threw themselves down on their knees and begged to be pardoned. Luckily for them, the good vibes of Augusta's birth had clearly infected everyone, and they were allowed to go on their way with a stern reprimand as their only punishment.

Yet all wasn't wine and roses during the early years of the two princesses and George was plagued by challenges from Parliament and further afield as he battled to keep the ship of monarchy steady. Though not yet afflicted by the mental illness that would later cause him so much pain, he felt every slight challenge deeply and Charlotte, his devoted wife, decided that he needed a distraction. Having been inoculated against the scourge of smallpox the previous winter, Royal was thriving, and Augusta charmed everyone who met her, so Charlotte came up with the idea of holding a drawing room hosted not by her husband, but by her children.

The drawing room that Charlotte envisioned was actually a reception at which members of the court could gather to meet the king. Charlotte, well aware of the political manoeuvrings that her husband was facing, thought that it would be a jape to have the seven-year-old Prince of Wales and the three-year-old Royal take her husband's place and receive his illustrious guests. Charlotte had an ulterior motive too. She hoped that the king's opponents would see how devoted he was to his children and that this would cause even his most hard-hearted enemies to thaw. Idealistic, perhaps, but very Charlotte.

On 25 October 1769, the anniversary of George III's accession, the children were duly installed in pride of place in St James's Palace. The *Whitehall Evening Post* painted a vivid picture of the scene.

> 'On Wednesday night the Prince of Wales and young Princes, with the Princess Royal, had a Drawing-Room. For the first time, in the Princess Amelia's late apartments. The Prince was dressed in scarlet and gold, with the ensigns of the order of the Garter; on his right was the Bishop of Osnaburgh in blue and gold; with the ensigns of the order of the Bath; next to him, on a rich sopha [sic], sat the Princess Royal, with the other Princes to her right, elegantly dressed in Roman togas. The sight of so many fine children, all of one family, their great affability, and the recollection of their dignity, gave the most pleasing impressions to everyone present.'[14]

The Bishop of Osnaburgh, or Osnabruck, was little Prince Frederick. At just six years old, he was already more highly decorated than some of those fawning courtiers would ever be, and how this must have chafed. No matter what they might have really thought, no one present could risk appearing anything other than utterly enchanted by the sight of the little royals as they presided over all they surveyed. Outside the environs of the palace, however, things weren't quite so glowing.

The idea of this folly was a gift to the caricaturists and one particularly vicious work mocked the absurdity of the court being received by a nursery's worth of royal children. In a caricature that was circulated after details of the event were made public, the young Prince of Wales is shown playing with a kite, his ceremonial sword and wig oversized and ridiculous. Prince William ignores the scraping courtiers in favour of his spinning top and the illustrious infant Bishop of Osnabruck is more concerned with his hobby horse than his adoring attendants. The young Princess Royal, meanwhile, was depicted secreted behind a screen, being comforted by her wet nurse.

Despite the barbs that were aimed at her unusual experiment in public relations, Queen Charlotte decided that she would give it another go. The following year the Prince of Wales hosted a juvenile ball. This time, however, Royal wasn't on co-starring duties.

To the outside world, it must have looked as though the royal children had the most perfect lives, yet for Wales and York in particular, everyday life could be trying. They were subjected to a rigorous educational regime that occupied hours each day and was focussed on forging them into the humble, pious, regal boys that their father believed they should be. There was little room for anything beyond disciplined learning and prayer and the boys loved the moments when they could escape outdoors to tend their plots of earth, where they grew vegetables much to the delight of the king, who was so keen on agriculture that he earned the nickname, *Farmer George*. Should they step out of line the boys were beaten by their tutors, in the belief that this alone would force them to behave in a suitably princely fashion. In the case of Wales, of course, it did anything but.

> 'Tuesday morning between eight and nine o'clock, the Queen was happily delivered of a Princess. Her Royal Highness the Princess Dowager of Wales, his Grace the Archbishop of Canterbury, several Lord of his Majesty's most Hon. Privy Council, and the Ladies of her Majesty's Bed-chamber, were present.
>
> Her Majesty is, God be praised, as well as can be expected; and the young Princess is in perfect health.
>
> The event was immediately made known by the firing of the Tower guns.
>
> [...]
>
> We hear her Majesty had a very favourable time, being only a few minutes in labour.
>
> Dr Hunter delivered her Majesty.
>
> Last Tuesday caudle was given at St. James's, on the happy delivery of her Majesty, and will continue for some days, as usual.'[15]

The royal daughters might reasonably be said to have arrived almost in batches of three. The first trio was completed by the safe delivery of Princess Elizabeth, named after her father's sister, who had died at the age of just 18. Elizabeth was brought into the world by Dr Hunter on 22 May 1770, bringing the tally of royal children to seven.

Charlotte and George weren't even halfway finished.

9

The First Trio

'They are indeed uncommonly handsome, each in their different way – the Princess Royal for figure, the Princess Augusta for countenance, and the Princess Elizabeth for face.'[16]

Royal was no longer the only girl in the nursery and Lady Charlotte Finch was in need of another pair of hands to help her marshal her charges. Following the birth of Princess Elizabeth, Mary Dacres, was appointed to join the ever-growing team as dresser to Royal and Augusta. The job of wet nurse went to Mrs Elizabeth Spinloffe. Queen Charlotte's accounts confirm that, like Mrs Muttlebury and Mrs Thursby before her, Miss Spinloffe was placed on a salary of £200. As the years passed, Lady Elizabeth Waldegrave was added to the household as Lady of the Bedchamber to the Princess Royal, with whom she became close friends. When Lady Elizabeth's mother, Maria, secretly married George III's brother, Prince William Henry, she became far more besides.

Although Miss Dacres was soon a firm favourite of her little charges, it's important to note that these weren't abandoned royal children who were farmed out to the care of attendants. Unlike their Georgian predecessors, George and Charlotte were engaged parents and though the stern Charlotte sometimes managed her offspring like a team of staff rather than children, George was a little more lenient. Not much, but a little. He loved to spend time with the children and truly valued their uncomplicated company as they played indoors or roamed the grounds together. Though their life was one of discipline, it was also more private and domestic than that of their predecessors had been.

Though George I had been estranged from his son, George II, and George II had in turn been estranged from his own eldest son, Frederick, George III's late father, George III himself was determined that his own children wouldn't suffer the same fate. It was an honourable aim but one that ultimately wasn't to be.

To this end, George and Charlotte were determined to ensure that their children would have childhoods on which they could look back with fondness – other than the occasional beatings, of course.

Yet what they couldn't guard against, no matter how hard they tried, were the opinions of others. For a girl in the eighteenth century, particularly the daughter of a king, marriage was a foregone conclusion. It was with this eventual aim in mind that the princesses were educated and studied the necessary *feminine arts* such as dance and illustration, the latter under Thomas Gainsborough, no less. For all this schooling though, it was a hard fact that intelligence would only carry the princesses so far. They had to look the part too.

When Lady Mary Coke paid a visit to the see the children in their home of Richmond Lodge, she declared that Royal was 'far from pretty'. At just five years old, she had already been found wanting. Even Augusta wasn't spared Lady Mary's critical eye and she lamented that the second princess was 'rather pretty, but not so well as she was last year'. From the distance of two and a half centuries we might gnash our teeth at Lady Mary's unvarnished truth but for the girls, looks were one more necessary part of the package and Lady Mary was never one to mince her words.

Nobody else did, after all.

The girls were regarded as the three most eligible young ladies in Great Britain and when they made a public appearance, they did so as a matching set. The youngest even 'dressed alike, nearly in the same manner as the *Princess Royal*,'[17] three peas from the same royal pod.

But not all of them were happy there.

Family Crises

In our jaunt through the adventures of the daughters of George III, one thing we can be sure of is that the princesses didn't exist in a vacuum. Their lives, such as they were to become, were shaped by the events that George and Charlotte faced during the monarch's turbulent reign. Though George valued his life at home and tried to be engaged with his children in a way that his predecessors never had been, away from the family's private drawing rooms things were far from easy for the king.

George was not a born politician and though it was a skill he tried to master, it was never one that came easily to him. Always a man with delicate nerves, his opponents knew how to jangle them and once jangled, George found it hard to compose himself again. He fretted and dwelt on matters of family and politics and the more trouble he had to deal with, the more determined he became that his own children would be raised in the cocooned safety of a protective bubble. This wasn't cruelty either, but the actions of a father who honestly believed that it was the only way to ensure that his daughters remained protected from the pressures and reality of the world at large. Instead they were to be forever clutched to the royal bosom, cossetted and isolated in equal measure.

As life in Great Britain rolled on, George's attentions were hovering somewhere between Westminster and North America. He did battle with the Stamp Act, with the ruinously expensive aftermath of the Seven Years' War, with the almost revolving door of the House of Commons, and with the growing and vocal dissent on the streets of America. The year before the birth of the Princess Royal, George had experienced his first significant episode of ill health and it had left him shaken. It began that January when George 'had a violent cold, had passed a restless night, and complained of stitches in his breast'[18], but the episode seemed to pass without growing any worse. Because this bout of ill health seemed to be a relatively brief and isolated incident, the notes were equally scant. They contained none of the sometimes gruesome details included in the eye-opening medical records that were assembled by Francis Willis, the doctor eventually brought in to treat George's mental illness. On this occasion, 'His Majesty was blooded 14 ounces'[19], and that was that. As we shall see, the king's health problems were far from over.

But even as Royal and her sisters were playing happily in the royal nursery, the king was fending off challenges from all sides. Though George didn't know it at the time, just three weeks before the birth of the Princess Royal was marked with caudle and ceremonial cheer, there had been another important development in the royal family. On 6 September 1766 George's brother, Prince William Henry, Duke of Gloucester and Edinburgh, had married Maria, the widow of the late Earl Waldegrave. The beautiful Maria was more than two decades younger than her late husband and had just turned 30 when she married Gloucester. Neither George nor anyone else was aware that the wedding had taken place and when it came out six years later thanks to *another* clandestine royal marriage, the fallout was immense.

The king was still labouring under the misapprehension that his brother remained a single man when Prince Edward, Duke of York and Albany, died. With only ten months between them in age, as boys,

George and York had been the closest of companions, best friends who guided one another through their father's early death, but over the years that had passed, they had grown apart. As George's destiny led him to a life of pious rule and respectability, York embraced the celebrity that came with his rank, and became one of society's most well-known and well-liked characters. His sudden death in Monaco at the age of just 28 was a blow to George and hot on its heels came more challenges for the monarch, adding to the burdens he already shouldered.

In Parliament, turbulence once again swept through the chamber. As the court mourned its late, lamented prince, in Westminster nothing could stop the relentless march of ambition. William Pitt, that famed political titan, had long been locked in a struggle with the king from which neither man emerged unscathed but when debilitating ill health felled Pitt in 1768, all it did was bring another of George's opponents to the fore. Pitt's indisposition paved the way for the administration of Augustus FitzRoy, 3rd Duke of Grafton, a man the king wasn't overly fond by any means. For the monarch, it was one more headache.

Following the death of his father, Frederick, Prince of Wales, George had been tutored and mentored by John Stuart, 3rd Earl of Bute, a long-time favourite of the king's parents after they met during an impromptu game of cards. Lord Bute's influence on the young Prince of Wales had led to accusations that he was the lover of George's mother, Augusta, and when he became Prime Minister for a short-lived term of eleven months in 1762, he found himself beset by accusations of nepotism. One of his loudest critics was the Duke of Grafton and now, with the latter at the head of government, George was forced to deal with him despite his personal distrust and dislike of the man.

Both Grafton and the king did all they could to encourage the ailing Pitt's recovery but, like George, he too was afflicted by *melancholy* in addition to physical symptoms. When we consider the stresses he was dealing with in his public life, it's little wonder that George was so keen on spending time in the simple company of his children. Pitt, a great orator and statesman, wrote pitifully to the king to beg that he be allowed to resign, and one can't help but wonder if in some unacknowledged part of himself, George rather envied him that luxury. Wedded to the nation as much as he was to his queen, for George III duty was a lifetime commitment.

But if George found the youngsters a balm in times of trouble, Queen Charlotte wasn't quite so charmed by the simplicity of her children. Though often portrayed as a devoted and maternal figure, she was the parent who did more than any other to instil a sense of duty into her children. Not for her indulgence and carefree romps in the nursery, let alone games on the hearth rug. She was a woman whose adherence to protocol and piety was unswerving. In 1775 she wrote to the governess of the children, Lady Charlotte Finch, and told her, 'if every body is well behaved, at the Queens House of the Female party I should be glad to see my Daughters on Wednesday morning between 10 and 11.'[20] Before your eyebrows hit your hairline, remember that this was the Queen of Great Britain. Even her children needed an appointment.

But George needed that childish distraction to save him from the concerns of running a country that seemed to always be clamouring for a pound of flesh. In 1769 George's brother, Prince Henry, Duke of Cumberland, was plunged into scandal when he was publicly sued for adultery by the notorious Lord Grosvenor. Lady Grosvenor, the lord's glamorous wife, had been caught in the arms of the prince on more than one occasion, and the couple had enjoyed saucy assignations in inns across the south east, where Cumberland employed a variety of bad wigs and even worse fake accents to divert gossip. It was to no avail because word soon reached the cuckolded husband and he launched proceedings against the duke. Lord Grosvenor– himself no pillar of respectability – won the case and was awarded damages of £10,000. It was a sum that Cumberland simply couldn't hope to pay.

And neither could the king. Instead, it was left to the nation to settle the scandalous debt.

But Cumberland wasn't done with scandal just yet and in 1771 he gave George one of the biggest shocks of his life. It began innocently enough when Cumberland sought an audience with his brother at Richmond Lodge. As they strolled together, Cumberland handed George a letter and the king must have braced himself for a fresh bombshell. If he suspected more trouble was on the way, he was right. Cumberland had learned nothing from his brush with scandal in the Grosvenor affair and had gone one step further this time, marrying a widowed commoner named Mrs Anne Horton. He begged for George's approval of the match but the king, to whom piety and fidelity were everything, was horrified. He turned his back on the devastated Duke of Cumberland, banishing him from court.

But George wasn't finished yet.

It was thanks to Cumberland's erring romantic ways that the king now introduced a piece of legislation that would echo through the lives of his children, both male and female, for decades.

The Royal Marriages Act of 1772 was a blunt instrument wielded by a king who believed he had run out of options and who wasn't and never would be able to accept that he couldn't dictate the love lives of his grown brothers. Everything they did seemed calculated to cause him offense and anxiety and as George's health problems later proved, anxiety was something that he was particularly susceptible to. His pleas to them to remember their place in society and behave accordingly went unheeded, so when all other avenues deserted him the king reached for his last resort. If his brothers wouldn't behave, he'd just have to force them to.

Although Cumberland was under no obligation to seek his sibling's permission to marry, good manners dictated that he should have done so. Though the letter handed over at Richmond Lodge was couched in the most careful terms, the king was furious at its contents. He ordered Cumberland to leave his presence and turned instead to Gloucester for some sibling support.

That was, lest we forget, the very same Gloucester who had been secretly married to Maria Walpole[21], herself illegitimate, for five years. Though her father was wealthy and her parents' relationship was loving, they had never made it official. That meant that in the eyes of the king and the upper echelons of society, a marriage between Maria and the duke was utterly unconscionable. As George raged about Cumberland's subterfuge and the disappointment and hurt the clandestine marriage had caused him, one can only wonder what was going through Gloucester's head.

Every time he thought of the possible consequences of an unwise marriage in his family, George's imagination ran wild. Soon he began to draw up ever more elaborate fantasies in which the Cumberland marriage plunged England back into the days of the Wars of the Roses, splitting the nation in half and dividing the loyalties of his subjects between the king and the Duke of Cumberland. His worries were calmed by Gloucester, who wisely decided that now wasn't the time to make his own admission. But he couldn't keep it a secret forever and when Maria fell pregnant in 1772, he could be silent no more.

As Gloucester was trying to find the perfect moment to tell his brother of his own secret marriage, George was formulating a plan that would put an end to the business of royals marrying commoners forever. Queen Charlotte, to whom reputation and protocol were everything, was one of her husband's strongest supporters when it came to matters of propriety. Their marriage was solid and faithful and importantly to them, socially appropriate. They were both royal, both dedicated to duty, and both determined that their family should follow their example. If they couldn't be trusted to do that off their own backs, then the only way to ensure that they toed the line was to enshrine it in law. To us this may seem bizarre, but one need only consider the interest aroused by some modern royal marriages to see that in some ways, the state of dynastic unions hasn't changed that much over the years. In fact, some even claimed that Charlotte liked to occasionally carp at her husband and remind him that George I's ill-fated wife, Sophia Dorothea of Celle, had been the daughter of Éléonore Desmier d'Olbreuse, a commoner. And look where that had ended up.[22]

Lord Dover recalled a dinner at Frogmore when, 'it was remarked that every person at the table was descended from the Electress Sophia [the mother of George I]; but the queen turned round, and, pointing to her heart, exclaimed proudly, 'Non, madame, il n'y a pas de l'Olbreuse ici.'' Charlotte might have been proud of her pure blood, but Lord Dover noted that, whilst he was glad that the queen 'derived such pleasure even from trifles; […] we are also glad that our royal race should possess this mixture of lower, but not therefore worst blood, which separates them more from the pedigree-hunting princes of the empire and makes them appear more naturally belonging to the mixed nobility and mixed government of this country.'[23]

Let Queen Charlotte crow all she liked, was the verdict, but *she* was the odd one out. There was not a family in England 'that could prove sixteen quarterings'[24], or that would be what is called Chapitrale. Even our present royal family are barred by the *sang d'Olbreuse!*"

Perhaps it was rare to find such a solid and unimpeachable history of noble marriages untouched by the blood of commoners, but the royal couple was willing to try. George and Charlotte were, as one historian put it, 'absolutely fanatic [when it came to] extreme notions as to the dignity conferred by birth and remote descent.'[25] These notions would have far-reaching consequences for more than one of their children and in the matter of the brides of Cumberland and Gloucester, there was no possibility that two commoners such as Anne and Maria would ever be considered as suitable brides.

George and Lord North, once his childhood tutor and now Prime Minister[26], put their heads together and between them came up with the Royal Marriages Act, which was precisely as much fun as it sounds. The act, written in typically impenetrable eighteenth century legalese, was more than political for the king: it was personal. He told Lord North that the Royal Marriages Act 'is not a question that immediately relates to Administration, but personally to myself; therefore I have a right to expect a hearty support from everyone in my service, and shall remember defaulters.'[27]

In other words, *don't let me down.*

And what was of such vital importance to George III that it must be enshrined in law? Simply put, the act required any descendent of George II to secure the permission of the monarch before they could marry. If the king withheld his consent, there was one scant hope open to those who were over the age of 25. In that case, they could give notice of their wish to marry to the Privy Council once the king's refusal had been received. Then all they had to do was wait for twelve long months and so long as neither the Commons nor the Lords objected, they could be married. Should any member of the royal family go ahead and marry without following the terms of the act, the marriage would be void[28] and should anyone assist a member of the family in undertaking such a marriage, they would be liable for prosecution. In cases where a marriage was undertaken without the consent of the monarch, any children born of that marriage would be exempt from the line of succession.

It's a measure of George and Charlotte's belief in the importance of what the public regarded as a ridiculous act that the monarch pushed it forward, ignoring the dissent of his subjects and some parliamentarians, who bemoaned it as a tyrannical attempt by the sovereign to control his family's personal lives. Even the efforts of the Duke of Cumberland, who came to the House of Lords to speak against the act, did nothing to move George and his precious Royal Marriages Act was passed in Westminster.

The act was given the Royal Assent on 1 April 1772. Two months before that, George suffered a great personal loss with the death of his mother, Augusta. She had been a divisive figure in public and Parliament, where rumours of her favouritism and malign influence persisted, but to George she had been an unflinching rock during the years of his fatherless adolescence. Her death from throat cancer was drawn out and agonising and George felt her loss very deeply. Now he was truly the head of the family. Mostly.

As 1772 wore on and George celebrated the passing of the Royal Marriages Act into law, he was also mourning the loss of his mother. Perhaps he hoped that this would be an end to scandal, but if he did, he was sorely mistaken. The funeral of the late Dowager Princess of Wales descended into chaos as protestors spat on the coffin of the king's mother and tore at the mourning drapery that adorned Westminster Abbey. Tired of what they saw as Augusta's devotion to cronyism and factionalist tendencies, they jeered and heckled her cortege as it passed through London. Several injuries were even reported as any sense of decorum went rudely out of the window.

> 'The funeral of her Royal Highness the Princess of Wales was very ill conducted on Saturday night; the mob were so numerous and insolent, that great part of the black cloth that covered the sides of the platform was torn off before the procession was half over, and the soldiers, instead of seizing or keeping off the offenders, only seemed desirous of sharing in the spoils.'[29]

But if these family schisms and heartbreaks made George a more attentive father, there was a storm brewing in Denmark that would eventually have a far less pleasant impact on the lives of the royal daughters.

Caroline Matilda, the king's sister who had given the Princess Royal one of her many names, was just 15 when she was sent off to Denmark to marry her cousin, Christian VII of Denmark. She didn't want to go, and she was ill-prepared to do so. Born four months after the death of her father, Caroline Matilda was raised away from the court and enjoyed a relatively simple life. Like her brother, George, she adored being outdoors, and also like him, the matter of her marriage was one that wouldn't be left to chance. When word went around that Christian was seeking a bride, the preferred candidate was actually Caroline Matilda's sister, Princess Louisa, but her ill health soon put paid to that idea. Instead it was Caroline Matilda who drew the short straw[30].

When Caroline Matilda arrived in Copenhagen she was plunged into a nightmare. A world away from her quiet upbringing, she found herself married to a husband who had no wish for a wife. Christian, who was two years her senior, preferred to spend his time in the capital's brothels than with his bride and when he *was* at home, his eccentric behaviour was rapidly becoming more and more disturbing. Under pressure from his ministers and court, Christian eventually performed his dynastic duties and Caroline Matilda duly gave birth to a son and heir, Frederick.

Yet the arrival of his heir did nothing to calm the king's strange behaviour and in an effort to rein in his eccentricities, Christian was eventually sent on a tour of Europe. It was during this tour that he met a Prussian doctor, Johann Friedrich Struensee. Struensee exhibited a remarkably calming influence on Christian and when the party returned to Denmark, the doctor came with them. He was soon a regular figure at the Oldenburg court, and at twelve years older than the sovereign, he was the only man who knew the cheat codes for Christian's troubled mind.

At first, Caroline Matilda thought little of Struensee. She was suspicious of his motives and ambitions but when he cared for her son during a deadly epidemic of smallpox, the stage was set for scandal. Neglected by her husband and ignored by the austere courtiers who surrounded him, Caroline Matilda fell hard for the Prussian doctor. As Christian's mental health grew more tortured, his queen and his physician embarked on a passionate affair that was soon the talk of the court. Despite this, the king continued to trust Struensee and gave him more and more power until he was a virtual regent, resulting in an era that became known as *the Time of Struensee*. It also resulted in a daughter who, though officially acknowledged as the child of the king, was widely believed to be the offspring of the queen and his physician[31].

Eventually and inevitably it fell apart in spectacular style[32]. Just two months after George had buried his own mother Struensee was found guilty of usurping royal authority and he was executed before a crowd of thousands. Caroline Matilda, the Queen of Denmark and sister of King George III, was placed under arrest. She too was charged with usurping the royal authority, the very crime for which her lover had been tortured and beheaded.

The queen was spared the scaffold but was instead placed under house arrest at Kronborg Castle. She wrote to her brother and begged him to bring her home, but George didn't. Instead he simply arranged her relocation to Celle Castle, hoping that distance would stop the scandal from leaking out.

It was a scant hope, for spiriting Caroline Matilda out of Denmark would have been a tricky affair that might have led to a diplomatic meltdown. At first, the press was filled with reports that a naval fleet was being prepared with the intention of bringing the queen home. Those reports soon darkened in tone, ascribing a far less charitable motive to that same fleet. Quite apart from rescuing the queen, said the newspapers, 'thirteen sail of the line, five frigates and bomb-ketches' were being prepared in Portsmouth and the 'destination of this fleet is no secret; it is being intended to lay the capital of Denmark in ashes.'[33] In fact there was no chance of war with Denmark and though acres of newsprint continued to be devoted to Caroline Matilda's confinement and fate, there was no shortage of attempts to silence the media, as demonstrated by the *London Packet or New Evening Post* on 10 April 1772.

> 'Several of the news-papers have been desired, from *above*, not to insert any thing further relative to the Queen of Denmark, for the present."

Fat chance.

And still the scandals came.

As 1772 gave way to 1773, Maria, the Duchess of Gloucester, was starting to look a little plump. Though a pregnant royal mistress was far from unheard of, Maria wasn't willing to have her reputation blackened by such a belief. She wanted her husband to come clean to the king. Well aware of the fate that had befallen Cumberland when he had confessed his own clandestine marriage to their brother, now it was Gloucester's turn to do just that. This time rather than simply banish him, George gave Gloucester a choice.

The duke could choose to be a husband to Maria and a father to their child, said the king, or he could choose to be loyal to the crown. What he couldn't do was have both. It was a terrible choice, but Cumberland went with the former. Just like Gloucester, he forsook his piqued brother and stayed loyal to his wife. The result was another banishing, leaving both George and Gloucester bereft as they parted ways. Given all this drama and all these reminders of the temporary nature of sibling affection, there's little wonder that George was determined to be a good father to his children. The loss of his own father at such a young age had also marked George's own promotion in the line of succession to heir apparent and with it, his adolescence became an endless routine of lessons in how to be king. There was precious little time to be a teenager. Life was duty, and duty was life. Such was the lot of George III.

As Charlotte, Augusta and Elizabeth grew and the years passed, the flurry of unsettled activity continued in the life of the king. Caroline Matilda never returned to England. She fell victim to scarlet fever in 1775 at the age of just 23 and her fate more than any other would haunt George. It ended up haunting most of his daughters too.

Just twelve months later in America, the Declaration of Independence sent a thunderclap across the Atlantic.

No wonder the king sought solace in the arms of his queen.

But it wasn't she who undertook the day to day care of the children.

The Governess

Lady Charlotte Finch, 'a woman of remarkable sense and philosophy'[34], was born in 1725 to Thomas Fermor, 1st Earl of Pomfret, and his wife, Henrietta. The couple were well-known at the court of George II and served in the household of Queen Caroline as Master of the Horse and Lady of the Bedchamber respectively. Lady Charlotte married diplomat William Finch and joined the royal household as a governess in 1762, immediately after the birth of the Prince of Wales. She would remain in her exalted position for more than three decades, enduring despite the death of two of her own daughters, her much older husband's mental instability[35] and even the breakdown of her marriage, following which she and her children took up temporary residence in St James's Palace.

The experienced and trusted Lady Charlotte managed a team of staff of her own, all of whom were devoted to the care of the youngsters. As well as Miss Cotesworth – of whom, more anon - Miss Frederica Planta taught the girls English and her sister, Margaret, stepped into her shoes following her death. Mademoiselle Suzanne Moula headed the team responsible for teaching the princesses French and notable among the other names is one Johann Christian Bach, who instructed them in music. Whilst the king devised a programme of education for his sons, it was left to Queen Charlotte to do the same for her daughters. For them, the aim was to create the very model of marriageable young ladies, fluent in languages - including the all-important French and German that would be indispensable for royal brides - and the arts, well-versed in history and able to converse both in writing and verbally on all manner of subjects. To put it bluntly, they must make excellent wives when eligible royal bachelors cast their nets.

No member of the household was closer to the children than Lady Charlotte, but despite her three decades of service and her intimate knowledge of the comings and goings of the royal family, she was still a servant. When Mrs Cotesworth left the royal employ under a cloud in 1774 it was left to Lady Charlotte to give her her marching orders. Though the reason behind Mrs Cotesworth's departure is shrouded in mystery, allegations of excessive drinking dogged her and if this was the case, then her removal from service is hardly a surprise. Yet whilst she might be responsible for doing the dirty work, when it came to recruitment, Lady Charlotte was expected to remember her place. She was reminded of this in a telling letter from the queen in which we can read between the lines and see that the governess had perhaps asked why she wasn't responsible for appointing the new sub-governess. It would only seem to make sense that Lady Charlotte should have some say in who would be joining her team, but the queen wasn't having any of it.

> 'My dear Lady Charlotte Finch,
>
> Nothing can give me more and greater pleasure than the manner in which you have finished everything with Mrs. Cotesworth. […] Let me explain some part of our Tuesdays [sic] conversation. You said that in coming into the Family you felt some distress in not having appointed the subgoverness. This I believe is a mistake as I find by the King that this place is not to be disposed of by either the Governor or Governess but by us alone, their recommendations are taken as well and in preference to others, but the choice and determination lies solely in us.'[36]

Lady Charlotte, the queen was saying in her polite way, should watch her manners. Later in the letter, Queen Charlotte dealt with the matter of the governess' more than reasonable request for two days off each week. Considering the number of children in her care by 1774 this was hardly unreasonable, but even though the request was agreed to, it was with conditions attached. Lady Charlotte, who was already in attendance on the children for six hours a day and all evening until the queen decided she could be dismissed, could have her two days only if she agreed to work even longer hours to make up for the shortfall.

> 'Nothing can be more just than the request you have made of having two days in the week of your own liberty to see your friends. I feel the happiness of such a comfort as much myself that I do enjoy it with you, but now on the other hand I must beg of you that the other days you will rather increase your own attendance upon the Children.'[37]

The governess was stunned. Although Lady Charlotte knew her namesake well enough to know that the queen would never change her mind on the matter of who would appoint the sub-governess, Lady Charlotte couldn't let it go unchallenged. She resented the implication that she might have a vested interest in any candidate and was keen to rebuff it.

> 'As to the Right of appointing the subgoverness [...] the Person with whom I must be so connected from my Place, should be One, whose Principles & Sentiments were known to Me to be such as I could recommend as correspondent to my own, nothing being so detrimental in Education as a Contrariety of Opinions in those that are to act together in so important an Undertaking. Therefore I assure your Majesty I did not mention it as a claim on any other Foundation but the Reason of the Thing, having really nobody I wish particularly to recommend.'[38]

Not only that, but Lady Charlotte was nearing 50 and she had given years of her life to the service of the king and queen, so she couldn't let Charlotte's response to her request for two days off go unchallenged. In fact, she threatened to resign. It was an empty threat though and the queen knew it.

> 'I am now by that Principle call'd upon to consider, whither I am capable of fulfilling according to your Majestys [sic] wishes & Intentions, the Commands you express of having

my Attendance increas'd on the other days. The Attendance I have hitherto given has been regularly a double Daily Attendance of two & oftener three hours in the morning & from before Seven in the Evening till dismiss'd by your Majesty, besides numberless Occasional & Additional Attendances; [...] & now as I advance more in Years & very much decline in Spirits, how can I without deviating from my own Principles undertake an additional duty of a kind for which I am conscious I am growing every day more unfit, as your Majesty must know - what an uncommon Stock of Spirits & Cheerfulness is necessary to go through the growing Attendance of so many & such very young People in their Amusements, as well as Behaviour and Instruction, besides ordering all the Affairs of a Nursery [...] I could sooner submit to resign my Office into the hands of any Person younger & more fitted for it, than to be the Smallest Obstacle to the full & compleat Execution of your Majestys [sic] Wishes about it.'[39]

But Lady Charlotte Finch was dedicated to her charges and over the years of their childhood, she was a constant in all their lives. Even better, when the new subgoverness, Martha Gouldsworthy, was appointed, Lady Charlotte had every reason to celebrate. Despite her protestations that she had no personal favourite amongst the candidates that wasn't strictly true. Lady Charlotte's personal favourite was none other than Martha Gouldsworthy.

One-nil to the governess.

The Family Grows

'Yesterday morning at seven o'clock Her Majesty was safely delivered of a Princess; on which account notices were immediately sent to the Lord Chancellor, the Archbishop of Canterbury, all the Great Officers of State, foreign Ministers, &c. At ten o'clock the same day expresses were sent off to all the Courts in Europe of the happy delivery of the Queen, and the birth of a young Princess.

The Queen was taken ill on Wednesday night about eleven o'clock, and the great Officers of State, &c. were sent for to Buckingham House; but her Majesty being much better by twelve, they all went home, (except Dr Hunter and the Queen's Midwife) but were sent for again this morning about six.

Yesterday there was a very great Court and Drawing-room at St. James's to congratulate his Majesty on the happy delivery of the Queen, and the birth of another Princess.'[40]

Another princess.

When Princess Mary was born in 1776 her eldest brother, the Prince of Wales, was already a teenager and a decade had passed since the birth of Royal, the first daughter to enter the nursery. She shared her name with her paternal aunt, who had died four years earlier after serving as the landgravine of Hesse-Kassel at the side of her brutish and violent husband, Frederick II[41]. Mary was the eleventh child of George and Charlotte and unsurprisingly by this point, the matter of raising the royal children was as smooth as the proverbial well-oiled machine.

In addition to her three sisters Mary could count a whopping seven brothers as her siblings. The older boys rarely saw their younger counterparts or their sisters and whilst they were variously being raised to go into the military or even to sit on the throne, Mary's prospects and those of the other girls were very different. Like her sisters, she was entrusted to the care of a wet nurse, Anna Adams, and was soothed in her cradle by one of the official *rockers*, whose job it was to keep the baby peaceful in her crib. Though the latest member of a large brood, the lives of the sons and daughters of the king were very different. The boys were in their own establishments with their own tutor and the girls were entrusted to the care of the erstwhile Lady Charlotte Finch. Their paths rarely crossed by then and they grew up in separate establishments, as though they weren't even members of the same family.

As more and more children came along, the routine continued as smoothly as it ever had. The food was simple and fresh, with little in the way of the decadent meals one might expect of a royal family, and life was run along strictly timetabled lines whether at Kew – which had become the summer haunt of choice following the death of the Princess

Dowager of Wales - or Windsor. The king and queen woke at 6.00 am. Two hours later, Royal and the older children joined them for breakfast in their apartments and at 9.00 am, their younger siblings would join the family party. When the elder children went into their lessons, the younger ones enjoyed garden time and some lessons of their own. After dinner, the family walked in the grounds if the weather permitted then, as the king and queen attended to their business, the children were settled for the night. Before going to bed they were presented to their parents once more, this time to wish them goodnight.

Rarely did the day depart from its familiar routine but on one occasion in 1776, it did so in surprising style. The king and queen took Wales, York, Royal, and Augusta to Wimbledon to visit a gentleman named Hartley, who had come up with an ingenious way to prevent fire spreading in buildings. After breakfast, they witnessed a practical demonstration that entailed a bed being set on fire. As the family watched, the bedcovers and bedframe went up in flames before they burned out. They were shown similar demonstrations on the stairs and curtains and as the fires on the ground floor were lit, the royal party went up to the room above, where they saw for themselves that the fire hadn't spread.

To us nowadays, of course, the idea of six members of the royal family pottering around a house that was periodically bursting into flame is unthinkable. To the intrepid Georgians with their love of innovation, however, it was a welcome break from routine.

And the routine was as ordered and drilled as a military exercise. Given the number of children involved, it had to be.

Across the ocean, far away on the other side of the globe, another military operation was taking place. This was the American War of Independence which, by the time of Mary's birth, had been underway for twelve months. Just a few scant months later, the Declaration of Independence would be signed, but none of this was allowed to infiltrate the lives of the royal daughters. Yet the king wasn't so lucky and as Queen Charlotte neared her due date in 1777, George was doing battle with the North American colonies.

War or not, Princess Sophia wasn't going to stand on ceremony. In fact, she wasn't going to hang around at all and less than half an hour after Queen Charlotte went into labour, she gave birth.

'We, your Majesty's most dutiful and loyal Subjects, The Lord Mayor, Aldermen and Commons, of the City of

London, in Common Council assembled, humbly beg Leave to express our unfeigned Joy upon the happy delivery of our most gracious Queen, and the Birth of another Princess; an Event which we consider as an additional Strength to the present happy Establishment in your Majesty's Illustrious Family, and as a further Security for your enjoyment of our excellent Constitution in Church and State.

Long may your Majesty reign the true Guardian of the Liberties of this free Country; and be the Instrument, in the Hands of Providence, of transmitting to our Posterity those invaluable Rights and privileges which are the Birthright of the Subjects of this Kingdom.'[42]

But in the years that followed joy would be tempered by sadness, plunging the royal household into melancholy.

Two Deaths and a Daughter

'[Prince Alfred was] the first child that their Majesties lost, which, according to the old saying of the nursery, rendered the Queen a proper mother, and it must be acknowledged that her Majesty was exceedingly affected.'[43]

So far, the household of George and Charlotte had been lucky with its children. A dozen had been born and not only survived but thrived. Royal might be given to a timid stutter – something that her governess was charged with training her out of – and Wales might be nurturing a love of the finer things in life, but all seemed calm. Nothing touched their regimented days and even as war raged in America, life for the royal children continued with its routine.

Two new princes joined the family in 1779 and 1780 respectively. From the start, Octavius and Alfred fitted into the established routine admirably. Again came the wet nurses and rockers and the girls were thrilled by their two new playmates. Yet in the eighteenth century having twelve healthy children was no mean feat. Having fifteen would prove to be impossible even for the king and queen of the United Kingdom.

The new entries to the nursery were a balm to their father, who had been left reeling by the death of his sister in faraway Celle and the war that he was slowly losing in America. For Charlotte, meanwhile, two more pregnancies simply meant more exhaustion. She had been almost constantly pregnant for two decades and with each new child, the physical strain grew harder to bear and the children themselves became weaker. Of course, she had the best doctors that money could buy, and her children had a phalanx of well-drilled attendants to care for them, but that was of little consequence to the queen's physical ability to go on following pregnancy with pregnancy as she had been doing.

Health in the Georgian era was something that nobody could take for granted, whether prince or pauper, and smallpox was one of the most devastating scourges of the time. The royal couple had made it their business to have their older children inoculated against the illness and eventually the time came for their new siblings to follow suit. There was nothing untoward about this and George and Charlotte had no reason to suspect that the procedure wouldn't pass as devoid of drama as before. In fact, they didn't only have their children vaccinated but they took it upon themselves to have their household vaccinated too, as Queen Charlotte's assistant keeper of the wardrobe, Charlotte Papendiek, recalled in her memoirs.

'It was settled that Prince Ernest, her Majesty's brother, Prince William, and myself should be inoculated. I was taken to the Queen's house, there held by my father on one chair, the Prince by his nurse on another, their Majesties being present. It was first performed on Prince Ernest, then on myself, then on Prince William, after this manner: two punctures in the arm near to each other were made with the point of a lancet, through which a thread was drawn several times under the skin, and this on both arms. The operation was performed by Surgeon Blomfield, and was one of smarting pain, for we both cried. I was taken home in a sedan, kept warm, and in a few days had a convulsion, fever, and the pustules inflamed. On one arm they rose and dried off regularly. Prince William had pustules besides those on the arms, no convulsion, and was less ill, which was attributed to the female constitution being more delicate. On Prince Ernest it took no effect whatever. On our ultimate recovery all was considered right, and that we were secure from further fear of disease.'[44]

Not long after he had been inoculated, Alfred fell ill. With his parents away undertaking a tour, Lady Charlotte Finch took the little boy to Deal Castle where he was expected to take the waters until he was sufficiently recovered to return home. Yet as the days passed, Alfred showed no signs of recovery. In fact, his condition began to grow worse. With fears growing that he may have contracted the dreaded smallpox, little Alfred returned to Windsor. It was there that he died on 20 August 1782, just a month shy of his second birthday.

The king and queen were devastated but for George there was one small, perhaps odd comfort. He loved his son, of course, but his favourite child was Octavius, and he wrote, 'I am very sorry for Alfred, but if it had been Octavius, I should have died too.' The words were to prove as prophetic as they were heartfelt.

The month after Alfred's death Charlotte took up her pen and wrote to her son, William, future Duke of Clarence[45], by then far away from home and sailing as a member of the Royal Navy, to describe the horrible events that had passed.

'[Alfred's] strength decreased Daily, and this dear little suffering object dyed [sic] the 20ᵗʰ of August about five a clock in the Evening. This event though foreseen was a very trying one for the king, myself and every Body about us […] this little Angel now is far happier […] yet must I own my weakness, that I do feel a certain want of something which I cannot find. Providence has been uncommonly Gracious to me in every Respect and particularly in that of preserving me a large Family and even in this Stroke He was singularly Gracious, for it was the Youngest and least known of my children He deprived me of.'[46]

Seen now, many years later, it's easy to read this letter as somewhat dispassionate yet let's not be ungenerous to Charlotte. She was a woman to whom shows of emotion were not the done thing. Not placid by any means, she was steely if anything, but she was still a royal wife. A queen, in fact, regal and self-contained and dealing with one of the biggest losses any parent could face. Worse still, Alfred had begun to rally before his steep decline. There had been, if only for a moment, a glimmer of hope. Yet that hope was short-lived, and the death of Alfred was the first of two tragedies. The second would shatter the king into a million pieces.

Alfred's death left Octavius as the youngest prince and George doted on him all the more. He was also extraordinarily fond of the youngest of his daughters, Sophia, who playfully referred to her younger brother as her own son. The little girl was just fifteen months older than Octavius and the two were happy playmates, delighting their parents with their childish joy. The death of Alfred marked the first time that any of the royal children had fallen dangerously ill and it brought home to the household just how fortunate they had been over the years. Sadly, as we shall see, it wasn't to be the last bereavement to afflict the family.

Though Alfred had fallen victim to smallpox, the king and queen reasoned that the risk of losing another child to the infection far outweighed the risks inherent in having little Octavius vaccinated. With that in mind, Sophia and her brother underwent the procedure. By this time, Octavius was four years old and the queen, by now aged 39, was pregnant with the child who would be the couple's last. It was her fifteenth pregnancy and having spent much of her marriage either pregnant or recovering from childbirth, we can only imagine the strain this must have put on her. Yet that strain was about to increase.

Octavius and Amelia

Prince Alfred's decline after his smallpox vaccination had been slow and gradual, allowing the family the devastation of seeing their hopes for his recovery dashed. When Octavius fell ill on the other hand, his decline was swift. In April 1783 the king and queen were due to take a trip to Windsor when their youngest son suddenly became unwell. Remembering the agony of Alfred's fate, they postponed their planned journey and stayed with Octavius at Kew. The little boy died that same evening. He was the second of their children to pass away in the space of ten short months.

> 'On Saturday last, about Eight o'Clock in the Evening, died his Royal Highness Prince Octavius, his Majesty's youngest Son, to the great Grief of his Majesty, and all the Royal Family.'[47]

The little prince's death shattered the family. There had been no time to prepare for the worst, no clue of what was to come, just a sudden and shocking decline over the space of a couple of days. Those two youngest boys had been a welcome distraction for George from the troubles in America and now they were dead, cruelly snatched away before they'd had a chance to flourish. Unlike Alfred, however, Octavius appears not to have fallen victim to smallpox, although many at the time thought he had. It seemed as though the timing of his death, so close as it was to the vaccination, was simply an unpleasant coincidence.

The death of Octavius hit the king particularly hard. Horace Walpole recalled that George had commented that 'many people would regret they ever had so sweet a child, since they were forced to part with him: that is not my case; I am thankful to God for having graciously allowed me to enjoy such a creature for four years.'[48] Yet though there may have been some scant comfort in having known Octavius at all, the king was broken by grief. The queen, meanwhile, pinned all her hopes on her remaining children. As we shall learn in this volume, there was little room for manoeuvre or mistake in her ambition. Queen Charlotte's standards were so high that it would prove almost impossible for her daughters to ever meet them. In a letter to her son, William, she wrote:

> 'May it please the Almighty to preserve those that remain, and that they may prove to be Good Christians and useful Members of Society, this is the greatest Ambition, and I hope that this my wish will not fail to be fulfilled.'[49]

George tried to assuage his grief by finding a new favourite and he clung to the couple's last and youngest child, Princess Amelia, who was born on 7 August 1783. Over the precious few years of her life she became one of George's closest and most treasured allies. Her death was the catalyst for her father's final, fatal decline.

> 'Yesterday morning, at half an hour after two o'clock, her Majesty was safely delivered of a Princess, (and not a prince as mentioned in our last by mistake) at her lodge at Windsor; an express arrived at twelve o'clock, at the Secretary of State's office, with an account of the above great event, which was immediately announced to the Public by the firing of the Tower and Park guns. Her Majesty and the young Princess, at the time the express left Windsor, were as well as could be expected.
>
> Dr. Ford attended her Majesty, having succeeded to that high honour by the death of the late Dr. Hunter.[50, 51]

In her memoirs, Charlotte Papendiek recalled that on this occasion 'caudle and cake were given to the public at Windsor only, another evident mark of economy'[52]. However, whilst it's certainly true that the royal couple was noted for their relative frugality, that may not have been the reason behind this more subdued celebration. When Octavius died his young age meant that there was no official mourning for him but among his family, the grief was intense. Though Octavius' death certainly hit George the hardest of all, everyone in the household was devastated and it's not beyond the realms of possibility to imagine that there was little appetite for huge celebration among the family precisely because they were still mourning his loss. Instead they did just enough to celebrate Amelia's birth, but not so much that it might have been an affront to the treasured memory of the late prince. Amelia's godmothers were her own elder sisters, Royal and Augusta, making the birth of the new princess a distinctly domestic affair.

Amelia would come to be known affectionately as *Emily* by her family and her birth, coming as it did so soon after the death of her brother, did much to restore spirits. She made her first public appearance at just nine weeks old when the king presented her to the Duchess of Portland following a concert at Windsor. Few could recall a royal household that so clearly rejoiced in being a family as much as this one, with more than a dozen children and a devoted husband and wife. That wouldn't last.

So now we have all of our girls, with sixteen long years separating the eldest from the youngest. We have a king with a recurrent mental illness and a strong-willed queen who didn't like to be alone, not to mention princes to whom gadding about was a way of life. Throw in a nation that had lost America and a political climate that was choppy to say the least, and the years ahead were to be tumultuous indeed for the daughters of George III.

It's time to see what became of them.

Act Two

Charlotte, Princess Royal
(29 September 1766 – 5 October 1828)

The Young Royal

Charlotte, Princess Royal, was the first daughter and fourth child of George III and Charlotte of Mecklenburg-Strelitz. It was she who Lady Mary Coke had pronounced 'far from pretty' in her infancy, but what she may have lacked in looks, she more than made up for in intelligence. Royal was a fiercely bright and inquisitive student and discovered her passion for botany thanks to Lady Charlotte Finch, who first introduced her to the science in the gardens of Kew. She was also a talented artist who studied under no less a man than the celebrated portrait artist Benjamin West and her pen and ink drawings of wild animals can still be seen in the Royal Collection, demonstrating a lightness of touch and an eye for detail that is a mark of true talent. Indeed, her father recognised and respected her intelligence from the start and when a visitor admired the painted ceilings at Windsor, George called for his eldest daughter and asked her to 'explain the allegorical figures on the ceiling, which she did, blushing a little at first in the sweetest manner, with a distinct voice, and great propriety in her emphasis.'[1]

Subject to the strict educational regime of her parents, Royal's life wasn't one that we might immediately imagine when we think of the powdered hair and glittering jewels of the Georgian court. Instead she lived a rather austere lifestyle, in which strict routine was everything. She spent most of her days with her mother, who controlled the princess's daily routines, ensuring their food was plain and their education carefully monitored. On the plus side, unlike their brothers the girls were at least spared the beatings that were meted out as punishment for bad behaviour or insolence in the schoolroom.

Regardless of her own ambitions, Royal was expected to function as her mother's surrogate wherever necessary and monitor the behaviour of her younger sisters. They in turn came to regard her as something of a killjoy who was always ready to tell tales on them should they step out of line. Like Queen Charlotte, the Princess Royal could be bad-tempered too, and on more than one occasion she found herself having to write letters of apology to her attendants for some wrongdoing or another. She always had to be quick penning those remorseful letters because as evidenced by this note written to the queen by her attendant, Mary Hamilton, Royal wasn't the only one capable of telling tales.

> 'Miss Go[u]ldsworthy is much dissatisfied with Princess Royal's conduct, and, I am sorry to say, it is far from amiable. I am on very good terms with her, and have taken the liberty to represent to her that unless she corrects herself in time the Queen will grow indifferent about her; and scarcely a greater misfortune can befall her.'[2]

At 15, the Princess Royal wasn't above being dropped right in it. The erstwhile Miss Martha Gouldsworthy referred to in the letter became known to the girls as *Gouly* and was a subgoverness as well as one of the princess's favourite and most loved attendants. Sadly, even she couldn't guarantee their good behaviour.

It's interesting to note the threat of Queen Charlotte becoming *indifferent* as a punishment. So insular was the world the princesses were forced to inhabit that such a fate would be regarded as terrible indeed, leaving them further isolated within an already cloying world. Withdrawing her company from her daughters was a weapon the queen deployed whenever she felt piqued, because she knew they would always come to her on their figurative hands and knees. They dreaded incurring her wrath and she was quicker to lose her temper than she was to forgive.

Royal, however, had no love for the unofficial role of her mother's enforcer. The queen had a volatile temper which 'hourly grows worse, to which [Royal] is not only obliged to submit, but to be absolutely a slave.'[3] In the years to come, this resentment would grow ever more pronounced.

This might not have been a life of frippery and joy, but Royal was very much part of a loving family and the king and queen tried to spend time with their children every day. There was time for affection and silliness among the lessons and the household was a family home in a way that would have been unthinkable to George I and George II, who had been estranged at worst and icy at best. Relations had been equally chilly between George II and his son Frederick, Prince of Wales. Frederick was George III's father and he died when his son was still an adolescent. Left to be nurtured, and some might say dominated by his mother, George III never forgot how unexpectedly his father had been snatched away. He was determined that he would be present in the lives of his own children as long as he lived, following the example of his mother. Whether Charlotte nurtured or dominated we shall soon see.

The life of the Princess Royal was one that had been mapped out since birth. Although George III was never particularly robust, the worst episodes of his mental illness didn't surface until Royal was already a young woman and by that time, she had been ably prepared for the dynastic marriage that her parents intended her to one day make. She alone escaped before the storm.

Overtures from Brunswick

In 1782, the first overtures were made for the Princess Royal's hand in marriage. They came from Princess Augusta, George III's sister and herself the Duchess of Brunswick via her marriage to Charles William Ferdinand, Duke of Wolfenbüttel. Though she would eventually succeed in marrying off her daughter, Caroline, to the Prince of Wales and in doing so created one of the most disastrous unions in royal history, this wasn't the only marital scheme that Augusta envisioned. She was feeling rather flush with success having negotiated the marriage between her daughter, Augusta, and Frederick, Hereditary Prince of Württemberg, and she was ready for another challenge. Nobody could have guessed that this was that same Frederick who would later marry the Princess Royal too.

But with Augusta and Frederick safely married and out of her hair, the Duchess of Wolfenbüttel now turned her attention to her eldest son, Karl Georg August. The prince was just a few months older than Royal, but he had been born almost blind and with limited mental capacity and the thought of letting Royal marry him was abhorrent to both Charlotte and George. The king wrote to his sister and informed her that Royal, at just 16, was still in the midst of her education and that she wasn't yet ready for marriage[4]. Augusta wasn't convinced but she knew as well as anyone that once George had made up his mind, nothing would change it.

But the Princess Royal had more pressing matters to deal with. By now a young woman, she was ready to make her mark on society and she did it with a splash in 1782, when she attended her very first court ball. Her father, labouring under the symptoms of ill health that would eventually consume him, was not present to witness her moment in the spotlight.

For any young princess a first ball was a rite of passage and Royal opened the dancing at 9.00 pm with her brother, the Prince of Wales. Whether she knew he had called her 'a bandy-legged bitch'[5] in a letter to his mistress, Mary Robinson, just a year earlier, we do not know. I think, on balance, probably not.

Royal was resplendent in a white and gold gown that glittered with jewels, but as she began to dance, calamity struck. Her shoe buckle became somehow entangled with the fringe on her ornate petticoat and snatched her shoe right off her foot. Never a particularly limelight-loving kind of gal, the princess was mortified. Everything stopped so she could recover her shoe and before you could say 'buckles,' a Georgian wag had composed a whole song about the incident. I'll spare you the full four verses, but here's a little taster.

> ''Twas at the birth-night ball, Sir,
> God bless our gracious Queen,
> Where people great and small, Sir,
> Are on a footing seen;
> As down the dance,
> With heels from France,
> A royal couple flew,
> Tho' well she tripped,
> The Lady slipped,

Doodle, doodly, doo,
The Princess lost her shoe;
Her Highness hopp'd,
The fiddlers stopp'd,
Not knowing what to do.'

Happily, Royal recovered both her shoe and her composure, and the ball went on until well into the early hours. Following this memorable debut, she became a familiar sight at more and more official engagements, though always near her ever-watchful mother. As the queen once wrote to a duchess who dared to gad about while her children were in the sole care of their nurses, 'you are a mother; you now converse with a mother; and I should be sorry you would compel me to suppose you were callous where you ought to be most susceptible!'[6]

Ouch.

For the daughters of George III, there was to be no opportunity to strike out on their own, callous or otherwise.

Almost.

A Would-Be Suitor

The years came and went, and Royal's routine continued much as it ever had. There were trips to the coast, to the ball and theatre, there were outbreaks of measles and minor ailments but as the girl became a woman, there was precious little excitement. No more did the Duchess of Brunswick press her advantage but more worryingly as far as Royal was concerned, neither did anyone else. What was to be done if no suitor wanted the eldest daughter of a king? There were few young ladies *more* eligible than she was and yet she was so sheltered and hidden away from the world that still she remained on the shelf, as around her, society wedding bells were sounding.

There was this *one* chap though…

On 8 September 1787, an attorney named Thomas Stone wrote to Queen Charlotte and asked if she would permit him to marry the Princess Royal. This was no secret romance and certainly no fairy tale love story, but entirely a figment of his imagination. The letter he penned makes for an interesting read.

'MADAM,

WHEN I tell you that I am in a state of mental distraction, occasioned by the peculiar excellencies of your eldest daughter, I hope that you will pardon this presumption – Happy should I be, if my birth and circumstances could entitle me, legally, and according to the sanctifications of prudence, to demand the illustrious object of my passion; but as we are not responsible for our coming into this world, whatever we may be for our actions after that entrance, you must not blame me for not being a branch of the first house in Christendom. To come to the point - I have seen the Princess Royal; and must assure you, that the brilliancy of her beauties in the assemblage surpasses even the honours of her situation. - Though matrimony, in the present day, according to the ideas of Hudibras, is a mere matter of money, I reject so an idea; my affections are rivetted to the object of my desires, independent of advantages that may be presumed to be attached to her exaltation. It is true, that my estates at present are somewhat incumbered - but what of that? - the purity of my desires will operate as an antidote against the evils of poverty; I leave it to your discretion to mention the affair to his Majesty; you approve of the measure, I can have no objection. There is an old saying, that marriages are made in heaven; so, if this matter takes place, your Majesty knows, that the whole affair must be placed to the account of the Omnipotent, and not to the frail desires of a weak individual. Should Hymen illumine my being with his torch of connubial splendour; I flatter myself that we may live a VERY HAPPY COUPLE. In expectation of your Majesty's speedy answer.

I remain, with the most perfect veneration,

Your much obliged, most dutiful and devoted subject and servant,

THOMAS STONE'[7]

Stone was the son of a floor-cloth painter and had been born in Shaftsbury thirty-three years earlier. In his letter, he declared that he would be a fine suitor for the Princess Royal, having developed an ardent passion for her from afar. When he received no reply to his letter, he turned up at St James's Palace in the flesh and asked to be introduced to the princess. Sent away with a flea in his ear, he decided to head for Windsor. During his journey he heard that the royal family was in fact at Kew, so he made that his next stop. It was there that he was detained and taken to Bow Street to be questioned by Mr Bond, a Justice of the Peace, and Evan Nepean, the Under Secretary of State, as to his motives.

The press lost no time in reminding readers that it had only been the previous year that the king had survived a rather half-hearted attempt on his life by Margaret Nicholson, who wielded a knife with a blunt blade. She had been latterly confined to Bethlem Royal Hospital thanks to a plea for clemency from the uninjured monarch, so when Stone turned up at the royal gate in person, alarm bells rang. Of course, he might be nothing more than a hopeful if somewhat delusional chap but what if he, like Nicholson, had more violent business on his mind?

Though Stone believed that he and Royal would be a VERY HAPPY COUPLE, he was the only one that did. When he received no refusal to his proposal, Stone took that to mean that the king and queen were in favour of the idea and were ready to make wedding plans. At the time Stone was detained, his pockets were searched, and they were found to contain a bundle of love notes addressed to the princess. When questioned, he explained that he had fallen in love with some unknown woman three years earlier who he had determined just five months before his arrest to be the Princess Royal. It's more likely, of course, that three years earlier is the point at which his mental illness first began to convince him that someone had stolen his heart.

Whatever the timeline, it was a few months before Stone wrote to the queen, telling her that he'd encountered the princess and had become fixated on her. It had happened in March, he said, when he had been sitting in the two-shilling gallery at the theatre. The Princess Royal was seated below and at one point, she happened to glance up towards the gallery. Gripped by his delusion, Stone took that as a sign that they were soulmates and must be together at all costs. In that moment, he knew immediately who the woman who had stolen his heart truly was. Among the papers he was carrying was a love poem to the unfortunate princess, which read:

> 'Thrice glad were I to be your willing slave,
> But not the captive of the tool or knave;
> With woe on woe you melt my sighing breast,
> Whist you reject your humble would-be guest.'

Far from rejecting him, of course, Royal had literally no idea that Stone even existed. The attorney was committed to Bethlem on the request of the king and there was examined by the famed doctors of the Munro family. They concluded that he was mad and should remain under lock and key. Stone continued to write to the king in praise of his eldest daughter from Bethlem, none of which did anything to increase his chances of release. Instead he remained under lock and key in Bethlem for the rest of his life. He died behind the walls of the asylum in 1805.

King in Crisis

'I am quite charmed with the Princess Royal,' wrote Frances Burney in 1786. 'Unaffected condescension and native dignity are so happily blended in her whole deportment.'[8] Miss Burney was quite right, for Royal had been carefully schooled in the manner of princesses. She was no longer a girl and on the day of her twenty-first birthday, Frances Burney was present to witness the moment when Royal received her sisters, of whom she was 'affectionately fond', and was given gifts of a diamond necklace, portfolios for her artwork and a gold étui. All perfect presents for a princess.

At a time when the princess might reasonably be expecting to be looking to her own future, her mother instead appointed her as her botanical assistant. Steady, intelligent, and passionate about knowledge and her own improvement, Royal also functioned as a secretary for the queen but she was never particularly at ease in the company of her sometimes rather uptight mother. Of her father, however, she was as fond as all her sisters were, and when the king fell terribly ill in 1788, Royal was shaken to her core.

That summer, shattered by his battles with politicians and colonies alike, George III began to complain of stomach pains. They grew progressively worse and by the time autumn came, he was in the grip of madness. He barely slept and became increasingly violent, both verbally and physically, even going so far as to accuse Queen Charlotte of adultery. When the court physicians failed to calm her husband, Charlotte made the fateful decision to call in Francis Willis to treat him. This Lincolnshire clergyman turned doctor came highly recommended, having been widely credited with curing the madness of Lady Harcourt. Desperate to find an answer to her husband's malady, the queen welcomed him into her home. Willis' stock had never been higher.

With Willis treating the king at Kew, thoughts of anything resembling freedom for the Princess Royal were put aside. In the years to come, the king's struggles with mental illness would prevent her sisters from escaping the royal household. The Princess Royal, though she might not have felt it, was fortunate to be the oldest daughter in the family.

The Princess Royal's role as eldest daughter meant that she was chosen to accompany her parents to Cheltenham when a trip was prescribed for the king's health. George appeared to be recovering from his illness and in some respects perhaps he was, but in others he was still suffering terribly. The Prince of Wales was by now gadding about high society on the arm of Maria Fitzherbert, a twice-widowed Catholic woman who most took to be his mistress but who was actually his secret bride[9], and the king's mind was racing with this and other concerns. In an effort to fill his days and distract himself as much as possible, he devised an itinerary of outings that would have challenged even a healthy man, accompanied at every turn by his wife and eldest daughters.

For the Princess Royal, the trip to Cheltenham wasn't so much a break from the schedule as simply substituting one routine for another. By now in her early twenties, all around her Royal saw her friends and attendants marrying and striking out, but she seemed to be stuck somewhere in an adolescent limbo, still a girl in the eyes of her parents even though she was by now a grown woman. Yet how could this timid, reserved young lady ever voice her concerns when her family seemed to be consumed by constant drama? And what would her complaints do to the nervous king? Though he had professed to be feeling better during his trip to Cheltenham, George's health grew significantly worse after the family returned to Windsor that autumn. He ranted and raved more than ever until Charlotte was beside herself with despair. So bad did things get that as the king sank into insanity, Parliament began to consider the very real necessity of appointing a regent who could steer the kingdom during George's indisposition – however long it might last.

As the year drew on and Windsor was plunged into a freezing winter, the party moved to Kew. Here the king was straitjacketed by Dr Willis yet still he raved, speaking for hours on end, agitated, aggressive, angry, and certainly in no state to rule a realm. Yet in Parliament discussions dragged on and on regarding the proposed Regency Bill and the form it would take, not to mention who should be appointed as the caretaker of the kingdom. The obvious choice was Queen Charlotte, but she was too distressed by her husband's illness to consider it. What of the Prince of Wales then, the heir to the throne on the one hand but an ardent Whig on the other? The thought of their opponents gaining the upper hand in Parliament chilled the Tories to their marrow but as the politicians battled it out in the chamber, the king quite unexpectedly and very suddenly turned a corner.

George's behaviour had become so erratic at Kew that he had been mostly forbidden from seeing his daughters but from January 1789, they were once again admitted to his company. The king was far from well but he was at least mostly coherent again, for the first time in months. Across the country, celebrations were held to mark the sovereign's return to health and George, raring to get started on another project, began to muse on the prospect of travelling to Hanover. He conceived of a party, imagining a merry court gathering at which he could receive and vet possible German princes who might believe themselves to be appropriate suitors for his daughters. Sadly, it was not to be.

Doctor Willis ruled that George was not well enough for a trip overseas and told him instead that the furthest he should travel was Weymouth, where his health would benefit from the sea air. The king meekly obeyed and set out for the coast with his wife and the trio of eldest princesses. There were to be precious few eligible bachelors in Weymouth, but the girls could at least escape the same castle walls that had imprisoned them as surely as they had their father. Instead of Windsor they were to enjoy the surroundings of Gloucester Lodge in Weymouth, the summer residence of George's brother, Prince William Henry, Duke of Gloucester. They were no longer estranged, but George never allowed the scandalous duchess to be presented at court.

As the royal party headed south for the trip, everywhere they went they were met with crowds in the mood to celebrate. At Lyndhurst, the public watched as the royal family dined, then the party joined their audience in a bracing chorus of *God Save the King* and *Rule Britannia*. In a masterstroke of PR and much to the joy of the people who had gathered to toast the restored monarch, the family then strolled with their attendants through the crowds with cheers ringing out.

At every stop on their journey, the royal party was greeted by scenes of celebration. They were all deeply touched by the outpourings of joy and the receptions that had been dreamed up to demonstrate one thing and one thing only: Great Britain loved its king.

And it was just what the sovereign needed to see. As the family arrived at Weymouth they were met by the mayor at the head of a delegation of senior local officials, accompanied by a band playing *God Save the King*. The crowds roared their approval here just as they had all along the route from Windsor and to mark the royal family's arrival at Gloucester Lodge, the ships at anchor in the bay fired a twenty-one gun salute, which was answered by the battery on the esplanade. George, Charlotte and their daughters took a moment to survey the wide, open bay and the calm, vast expanse of the sea. The king, so recently raving and confined, told his wife, 'I never enjoyed a sight so pleasing.'[10]

To us it may seem a small thing for a princess to visit the seaside but for the daughters of George III, it was an eye-opening interlude. Visits to nobles punctuated trips to walk on the sand and bathe in the sea and with every new day, the king's health was restored that little bit more. Queen Charlotte, on the other hand, experienced some ill health of her own. Exhausted by her husband's struggles and laid low by the groundless accusations of adultery he made against her, not to mention his own lustful thoughts of her attendant, Lady Pembroke, during his illness, now the worst was over Queen Charlotte's constitution simply gave up. It was a short-lived malady though and by the time the family left Weymouth for Devon and another round of celebratory crowds and merry engagements, she was well on the road to recovery.

There was one unhappy incident that marred the trip and it came when the party travelled via state barge to Saltram. A vast array of vessels came out to greet them and the royal barges had scarcely left the reception when an overfull sloop capsized. The dozen passengers aboard were drowned. When news of the disaster reached the king and queen, they asked that all help be given to the families of the dead at the expense of the royal household. This was a king with a conscience.

The excursion to the south had a profound impact on the Princess Royal. As the family prepared to leave and return to its life of sequestered routine she remarked that, 'we never before had the pleasure of seeing nature in the perfection of beauty: our lives hitherto seem to have been spent in a cloister rather than in a kingdom abounding everywhere with lovely prospects, and inhabited by generous people.'[11]

And in those receptions, among the nobles who greeted them and the illustrious families who hosted them, might Royal have felt a little pang of longing for a household of her own, where she would be the one playing hostess, not simply the daughter who had yet to leave home?

If so, she was not the only one with plans for her future.

A Caller from Württemberg

In 1789, Queen Charlotte wrote of 'a very young man' who had expressed an interest in the hand of one of her daughters. He was Duke Ferdinand Frederick Augustus of Württemberg. A prince, no less. But if the drama in Denmark had convinced George that his daughter needed a better start than his sister had been given, Ferdinand might not be the man to provide it.

Ferdinand was the younger brother of Duke Frederick, Hereditary Prince of Württemberg. Frederick had been married to Duchess Augusta of Brunswick-Wolfenbüttel until her death in 1788. The late duchess just happened to be the sister of the unfortunate Karl Georg August, who had been rejected as a possible suitor for Royal years earlier. There were some considerable skeletons rattling in the closet of the marriage between Frederick and Augusta, skeletons that might suggest that the family from Württemberg wasn't one that the ruling house of Great Britain would want to get mixed up in.

The late Duchess Augusta was Royal's cousin, of course, as daughter of Princess Augusta, George III's sister. Augusta and Frederick were married in 1780 when the bride was just 15 and from the start, it was miserable. Though the couple had four children, three of whom would survive into adulthood[12], they were far from happy together. During a stay in Saint Petersburg in 1786, Augusta had abandoned her husband and thrown herself on the mercy of Catherine the Great, begging for protection from Frederick. She told the empress that her estranged husband was violent and kept a whole legion of young men as his lovers. Catherine, who had thought highly enough of Frederick to appoint him as Governor-General of Eastern Finland, was horrified. She asked him to leave Russia until the scandal had blown over and she agreed to assure Augusta's safety.

Frederick, however, was not about to go quietly. Packed off from Russia, he complained that it was not *he* who had behaved inappropriately, but his wife. Far from being the wounded party he declared that she had openly consorted with servants and stable boys. Banished and embarrassed, Frederick wasn't going to scurry back to Württemberg without having his say. He dismissed Augusta as a woman of poor moral character and left her in Russia just as she had wished. Though the couple were rid of each other, Augusta wanted to go one step further and be granted a divorce but her father, Charles William Ferdinand, Duke of Brunswick, wouldn't countenance it. It was one thing to be estranged, it was quite another to make the matter official.

With Frederick gone, Augusta was as free as she could hope to be and Catherine the Great gave her the run of Lohde Castle in which to live. Here she was to be watched over by Wilhelm von Pohlmann, one of Catherine's courtiers. Though he was nearly four decades Augusta's senior, the two were soon lovers and in 1788, Augusta fell pregnant by Pohlmann. Augusta went into labour that September and with her supposed guardian in no rush to expose his affair with his 23-year-old ward, Pohlmann didn't summon any help. Augusta's premature child was stillborn, and she died during the birth, leaving Frederick a widow.

As Frederick's brother, Ferdinand's lustre as a possible husband for one of the royal princesses was undoubtedly dimmed by his familial connection to the scandals in Russia. The rumours of bisexuality and abuse must have reached the ears of the court in England and though it wasn't Frederick who was being touted as the proposed bridegroom, the mud thrown at him had rather tainted the rest of the family. Let's not forget the debacle in Denmark, where George's own sister had married a man who we might charitably call *challenged*, a decision that had ended in scandal and death. If there were to be any nuptials amongst George's daughters, it was vital that the grooms came from respectable backgrounds and brought with them not the slightest whiff of controversy.

When George and Charlotte learned that Ferdinand wasn't interested in Royal but in her sister, Augusta, his efforts to impress in person by a visit to the court were summarily dismissed. It didn't matter how handsome the prince was, or how brave or decorated, or even how well-recommended he was by courtiers and nobles, all that mattered was that he had set his heart on the wrong princess. There was no chance that Augusta could marry before her elder sister. If there was to be a wedding, it must be the Princess Royal at the front of the queue.

It wasn't only Royal who was thinking of her marriage and in 1791 the Duke of York put forward a candidate for his eldest sister's hand – or the hand of *any* of his sisters - in the shape of Frederick William, Crown Prince of Prussia. York had become close to the prince whilst attempting to woo his half-sister, Frederica, and he hoped to keep it all in the extended family. Indeed, his wooing was to prove successful, because Frederica became his bride and the Duchess of York that same September, but for the Princess Royal and Frederick William, there was no such happy ending.

Royal was at the point of little caring *who* she married, so long as she married *somebody*. Though his plans for the Crown Prince took a back seat so he could focus on his own pursuit of Frederica, the seed had been sewn in Royal's mind. She began mentally sorting through a list of eligible men who were known to her and briefly settled on the Duke of Bedford, who she asked York and Wales to matchmake with her. At just a year her senior, Francis Russell, 5th Duke of Bedford, was a politician and an agriculturalist but he was also, crucially, a Whig. Perhaps Royal hoped the former qualities might endear him to her father but even if they did, his Whig allegiances would have made any proposed marriage impossible. For then at least, she was to remain withdrawn, lonely and dreaming of another life.

Duchess of Oldenburg

Royal was bored. Devoted to her husband's care and her royal duties, the queen was spending less time with her children and she wrote, 'I pity my three younger daughters, whose education I can no longer attend to,' but she had reckoned without the frustrations of the eldest. Queen Charlotte was embarked on a round of professional wifery, hosting noble visitors at Windsor and incurring the annoyance of Royal at doing so. The princess was tired of being her mother's administrator and of being forced to attend these visitors alongside her. She was tired, too, of being kept behind closed doors.

Since Charlotte was occupied with her husband and her visitors, Royal took it upon herself to look after young Princess Amelia and oversee her education just as the queen had done for her older daughters. Her father memorialised her dedication when he wrote an inscription to 'My Ever Dear Daughter Matilda [one of Royal's middle names], Governess to Her three Younger Sisters,' but as far as Charlotte was concerned, it was only what Royal's duty demanded of her.

Tired of the 'violence and caprice of her mother's temper', Royal began to look elsewhere for opportunities to achieve emancipation. By now in her early twenties, she asked the Prince of Wales if he would be able to find her a husband. No progress had been made on the king's idea to pursue his merry court in Hanover, nor to vet potential bridegrooms, and Royal was convinced that if she was to escape, then she must set the wheels in motion herself.

Wales pondered his sister's request, determined to help. He was devoted to her and knew all too well what sort of a life she could expect as their mother's go-to secretary and sounding board. He in turn discussed the matter with his brother and best friend, the Duke of York, and together the two princes began to consider who they might know who was single, willing, and suitable. There were, of course, some stipulations that must be met. First, the potential bridegroom must be of appropriate station to marry the eldest daughter of the British king. Second, under the terms of the Royal Marriages Act, he must on no account be Catholic. Last but by no means least, he must ideally be German. The House of Hanover had a long and established tradition of marrying into German royalty and with their German blood, it was a tradition that looked set to continue for the near future at least.

With Prince Ferdinand interested only in the prettier Augusta, he was off the list from the start. Very definitely *on* the list was Prince Peter Frederick Louis of Oldenburg, a member of the House of Holstein-Gottorp. Born in 1755, Prince Peter had served as the Regent of the Duchy of Oldenburg since 1785. He was respectable, reliable and had been left a widower by the death of his wife, Duchess Frederica. The Regent of Oldenburg also happened to be the Prince-Bishop of Lübeck and he wasn't a Catholic, but a Lutheran. Peter ticked virtually every box that the royal brothers might wish for and plenty more besides. More importantly, he ticked virtually every box that Charlotte and George might demand too. The only minor fly in the ointment was the fact that his late wife happened to be the sister of the supposedly abusive and bisexual Frederick of Württemberg, who you might remember had been drummed out of Russia, but this was hardly the sort of thing that could be held against him.

The king wasn't immune to efforts to find a match for his eldest daughter either. As a devoted husband to a devoted wife, he appreciated the benefits of a loving marriage and he knew all too well the hardships of depression and mental illness. George heard via his courtier, Sir James Bland-Burges, that Royal had 'fallen into a kind of quiet, desperate state, without hope, and open to every fear; or, in other words, what is commonly called, broken hearted.' He was worried for his daughter. When Sir Lucas Pepys, the Princess Royal's doctor, was called to attend the ailing young woman, he declared that the only medicine that would help her was marriage – quite a diagnosis for a Georgian doctor!

Put simply, it appears that Royal had succumbed to depression. She pinned all her hopes of future happiness on Peter, Duke of Oldenburg and wrote to Wales that, 'I am perfectly convinced that the Duke of Oldenburg's character is such that, could this be brought about, it would be the properest situation. [...] I shall leave it totally to you.'[13]

And Wales, crass, self-obsessed and selfish in most matters except the welfare of his siblings, did all he could to bring about the match. He wrote to his uncle, Prince Ernest of Mecklenburg-Strelitz, and begged him to contrive to bring Prince Peter with him to England so that he could meet the king and queen. Wales was sure that, if his parents could only get to know the respectable widower, they would consent to the marriage. Royal didn't know the prince herself, but she had come to a point where she longed not for love, but for escape. *The properest solution* was enough for her. She didn't need choirs of angels and rose petals and a storybook romance, just a home of her own and an adult life at last.

About to embark on his own doomed and miserable marriage to Caroline of Brunswick, perhaps Wales hoped that in doing a little matchmaking, he might see at least one happy royal marriage. He certainly did everything in his power to make Royal and Peter happen, short of dragging the prince across Europe by his ear and plonking him in front of the altar himself.

So excited did the princess become and so certain were her sisters that Wales could somehow conjure a bridegroom from Oldenburg that they began to teasingly call her *the Duchess of Oldenburg*. Elizabeth was thrilled at the very thought of it and said that, '[Royal's] maiden-blush is turned into a damask rose whenever the duke's name is mentioned'[14]. Then, just as it seemed as though nothing could prevent the match from going ahead, the trail went cold. Why the proposed betrothal was taken no further is a mystery, but we can well imagine how hard this must have hit the unhappy Princess Royal.

But all hope wasn't yet lost.

The Great Belly-gerent

Whilst the matchmaking efforts between the Princess Royal and Prince Peter went nowhere, quite unknown to her there was someone else hoping to secure her exceptionally eligible hand. The would-be groom was none other than Crown Prince Frederick of Württemberg, last seen leaving his estranged wife – George III's niece, let's not forget - in Russia amid a tangle of scandal and recriminations. There were rumours of brutality, of love affairs on both sides and latterly even of murder, with some groundless accusations flying around that the unfortunate princess had been murdered.

In late 1795 Frederick sent his representative to make a case for the marriage to Lord Grenville, Britain's Foreign Secretary. On paper there were some considerable plusses, not least of which was Frederick's direct lineage to Electress Sophia of Hanover, the mother of George I. There were also one or two negatives as well, especially the rumours of impropriety that had accompanied the breakdown of his marriage. The prince was physically unprepossessing too. He was enormously fat and had been nicknamed *the Great Belly-gerent*. Indeed, prints mocking his size and looks were soon sold across Britain once his interest in Royal became known. Even Napoleon got in on the act, claiming that God had created the prince merely as a means to test just how far human skin could be made to stretch!

Looks weren't of much importance to George III though. Instead, character was everything. When Grenville related the prince's matrimonial interest in Royal to the king, he was flabbergasted. He wrote to the Foreign Secretary giving an unequivocal reply.

> 'Knowing the brutal and other unpleasant qualities of this Prince, I could not give any encouragement to such a proposal. I therefore desire Lord Grenville will fairly tell him that I shall not consent to his request, and if he will not take a gentle hint, I have no objection to his adding that, after the very unhappy life my unfortunate niece led with him, I cannot as a father bequeath any daughter of mine on him.'[15]

George refused even to have an audience with the prince, determined to cut off the absurd plan at the knees before it had an opportunity to get out of hand. The king was not, however, a man without feeling so he sent agents overseas to find out the truth behind the rumours about Frederick's supposedly questionable character. George intended to discover 'whether my opinion on the Prince is well founded, which, if it is, no power on earth can get me to admit of his marrying a daughter of mine.' Yet what George learned from his agents surprised him and, satisfied that the accusations of brutality and murder might have been somewhat overstated, he began to rethink his decision.

Just as Royal might have given up hope, this unexpected ray of corpulent sunshine appeared on the horizon and George, once so dead against the Württemberg prince, began to change his mind. He was unexpectedly encouraged in his decision by his sister, Augusta, mother of the very woman to whom Prince Frederick of Württemberg had undergone such a miserable marriage. One might not have expected support for the prince from such a quarter, but she was probably focused on the wellbeing of her grandchildren who no longer had a mother.

Another point in his favour.

Royal and her father discussed the prince's interest and the king, mindful of her keen interest in marriage as a means to leave the family court, urged his daughter to take her time and consider carefully before deciding. After receiving intelligence from the continent, George's reservations were no longer about the man, but the perilous state of Europe. Eventually George decided that he would consent to the marriage but would only allow it to take place when he was satisfied that Germany was not about to be plunged into war.

The future now opened out before the Princess Royal and it was agreed that Frederick, who she had never seen, must come to England to meet her. Unfortunately, Royal was suffering from jaundice and was in no condition to receive visitors, but this suited George down to the ground – he was in no rush to see the back of her, after all.

As the princess began to recover, the king did all he could to delay the inevitable meeting. He instructed Frederick that he must not come to England until May 1797, as Royal suffered from seasickness and couldn't be permitted to travel any earlier than Spring. In addition, he instructed that Frederick's visit to the royal household would be of limited duration. After that he must take on an assumed name and travel the country, returning only when the time had come for the wedding itself.

It was an extraordinary and quite unnecessary bit of subterfuge and from the off, Frederick was having none of it. He travelled to England with no ceremony and arrived not in May, but as early as April. George was incensed, for Frederick made landfall not only before the marriage treaty had been signed off and returned from Württemberg, but before George had even had an opportunity to seek financial assistance from Parliament which eventually amounted to a dowry of an eyewatering £80,000. With the situation on the continent volatile, the money was to be invested in England and used to provide Royal with a yearly income. The king wouldn't risk losing it in the turmoil of Europe.

Yet George had hoped to set all of this in stone before his future son-in-law arrived. Nevertheless, the prince was in England and when Royal found out, nothing would prevent her from meeting him.

'On Saturday [15th April 1797], between twelve and one in the afternoon, the DUKE of WIRTEMBERG [sic] arrived from Chelmsford, with his retinue, at the Royal Hotel in Pall Mall […] and at half past seven o'clock went in the Duke of York's carriage to Buckingham House, where he was introduced by the Duke in form to Their MAJESTIES, the PRINCESS ROYAL, and the rest of the ROYAL FAMILY, with whom he staid till near nine o'clock.

His Royal Highness is of somewhat shorter stature, and more corpulent, than the PRINCE of WALES, but though fat, he is active, and well proportioned, of expressive countenance, and strongly resembles the Royal Family; his complexion is dark, and he has a large mole on his cheek; he appears to be about 40 years of age.'[16]

Frances Burney, always on hand when it came to relaying court gossip, wrote that Frederick did much to impress but that, 'the poor Princess Royal was almost dead with terror and affright at the first meeting. She could not utter a word. The Queen was obliged to speak her answers. The Prince said he hoped this first would be the last disturbance his presence would ever occasion her.'[17]

Smooth indeed, Frederick!

For Royal, 30-years-old and sure she was destined to be her mother's companion forever, the moment she dreamed had of for so long had finally come.

Queen Charlotte made the wedding dress herself, refusing help from all quarters as she made one last personal stamp on her eldest daughter's life. When the big day came, it was she who helped Royal into her gown. The couple was married at a glittering ceremony on 18 May 1797 in the Chapel Royal of St James's Palace. The groom wore an embroidered suit of peach and his bride 'a most superb and beautiful embroidery of white and silver; the body and train of silver tissue, trimmed with silver fringe.'[18] She was jewelled and primped and every inch the princess. It must have seemed like a dream come true.

In her journal, Frances Burney noted that Queen Charlotte had initially conceived of a gown of white and gold, as was traditional for a woman marrying a widower. The Princess Royal, however, was determined that she should be married in white and silver, as befit the eldest daughter of a king. On this occasion, at least, the opinionated queen decided not to argue. In some ways, this is a surprise but in others, perhaps we ought to give Charlotte a little slack. Royal was the first of her daughters to marry and the one who she had come to rely on but as the bride, it was only right that she be allowed the final say on her own wedding gown. Yet when Burney spoke to Princess Mary on the matter, the young woman told her that, 'you know what a figure [Royal] used to make of herself, with her odd manner of dressing herself; but mamma said, 'Now really, Princess Royal, this one time is the last, and I cannot suffer you to make such a quiz of yourself; so I will really have you dressed properly.' So perhaps not such a climb down for Charlotte after all.

A vast crowd gathered to watch the nuptials, and in the crush many members of the audience fainted clean away. Indeed, the bridesmaids themselves were nearly overcome by the temperature as they observed the emotional ceremony and came perilously close to swooning. The younger princesses wept openly, and George and Charlotte were clearly affected by the scene, which is hardly unsurprising given how close the family was.

The marital celebrations went on for days, with proclamations and drawing rooms, audiences and fetes coming thick and fast. The couple were showered with gifts including a ring for Royal specially commissioned by the queen. The ring contained thirty magnificent diamonds and Royal was lucky to get her hands on it at all, thanks to a hungry and rather cheeky chicken. Just days before the wedding as the trinket was being prepared by Mr Forster of Richmond Buildings, a chicken strolled into the shop and ate all but one of the diamonds that were intended for the ring. In doing so, the fowl signed its own execution warrant and the diamonds were retrieved from its intestines. Safely restored, the ring was sent on with a note that 'the chicken was too fond of rich bits!'

Two weeks after the wedding, the chicken-ring now safe once more, the time had come to depart. The bride and groom sailed from Harwich on 2 June, headed for the continent and new adventures. The family had said their tearful farewells the previous evening and the unhappy king and his eldest daughter had barely been able to bring themselves to end what would be their final embrace. Still, it was an excited and hopeful Royal who set off for her new life as the Crown Princess of Württemberg. On 12 June word was received at the Admiralty that the ship had safely docked at Cuxhaven after an uneventful voyage.

Charlotte, Princess Royal, was at last her own woman.

A New Life

The first ceremonial stop in Royal's new life was her ancestral land of Hanover, where she was greeted by her uncle, Prince Ernest of Mecklenburg-Strelitz, and her brother, Prince Adolphus, known to his sisters as *Dolly*. Here the newlyweds rested from their journey before they travelled on to Württemberg. They made for the family seat at

Ludwigsburg, where they were greeted by Frederick's family with all the ceremony and celebration that any newlywed royal might have hoped for. Though Royal never saw her beloved father again, her husband had a portrait of the king hung in her private rooms, which we must take to be a good sign for the years to come. With a reputation as a boor and a monster going ahead of him, Frederick was determined to make his wife happy in her new home.

When Royal married Frederick she became stepmother to three children, all of whom had left Russia with their father when the ill-fated Augusta remained as the guest of Catherine the Great. Contrary to the reports that had circulated of Frederick's bad behaviour, however, Royal found her new husband to be just as steady and reliable as she, if a little more intrepid when it came to riding out at speed and taking the odd tumble.

A few short months after the couple married, Frederick's father, Frederick II Eugene, Duke of Württemberg, died. Now Royal and Frederick were Duke and Duchess and Royal revelled in her role as the mistress of her own court. She was well-liked by her subjects and the royal family alike and soon the princess learned that she was pregnant. In late December 1797 the *Whitehall Evening Post* reported gleefully that, 'The Queen and Princesses are engaged at Windsor Lodge in working the furniture for a State cradle and other various articles of childbed linen, intended as a present to her Royal and Serene Highness the Princess of Wurtemberg, at Stutgard [sic].'[19]

Sadly, those handmade tokens were to go unused. Increasingly beset by the hard winter she was facing and the worry of war with France, Royal tried to keep herself busy and avoid dwelling on her worries. Just as Charlotte had soldiered on throughout her many pregnancies, now her eldest daughter attempted to follow that example and refused to be pampered. Just like her mother, she had duties to perform and with the death of the late duke and the pressures of her husband's new role, they were more numerous than ever.

By the time Royal's mother-in-law died in March 1798 the new duchess was on the verge of her due date and in England her youngest sister, Princess Amelia, was anxiously awaiting an 'account of the Birth of the little *Sprouting Branch*' from Württemberg. Winter turned to spring and snow to sunshine and Royal went into labour. Tragically, her daughter was stillborn. She was to remain childless to her death.

In a letter to her father, written soon after the death of her child, Royal reflected on 'the loss of the little thing I had built such happiness on,' but she was grateful for the attentions of 'the best of husbands and who, God knows, has suffered cruelly from his anxiety of my subject.' She tried to stay cheerful and to accept the loss as the will of God, but one can feel the sadness seeping from the pages of her letter. Grateful for the presence of her attendants and the understanding of her courtiers, Royal's thoughts were all for others. There was to be a ball given for the new arrival but when the baby was stillborn, the sponsor of the ball simply decided to hold it in honour of the duchess' good health instead. However, 'when [the sponsor] heard how deeply I was afflicted at the knowledge of the death of my child [he cancelled the celebration] for which I shall ever be obliged to him.'[20]

Yet we shouldn't underestimate the remarkable fact that Royal survived the stillbirth and recovered without complications. Though physically she was improving she remained heartsore and she took up her pen to tell the king, 'I can with truth assure you that at the moment I felt the most deeply the loss of my little angel; my heart and thoughts were also much taken up with what my dear parents would feel about me.'[21] She worried for others rather than herself. As her recovery continued, she became more active and was able to enjoy some fresh air as summer approached, but in her heart the daughter she had lost was never far away.

Perhaps it was this loss that led her to take such an interest in the niece who shared her name, Princess Charlotte of Wales. Charlotte was the daughter of Wales and his wife, Caroline of Brunswick, and though their marriage had been a catastrophe, they had somehow managed in the space of a just a handful of disastrous sexual liaisons to conceive a child.

Charlotte was born in January 1796 and was cared for by Lady Elgin, with whom Royal exchanged thoughtful letters on the matter of childrearing that offer a window into her personality. It's easy to see in those letters the unfulfilled longing of Royal for a daughter of her own and to see the phantom of the mother she might have been. Once rigidly schooled in preparation for marriage herself, Royal urged that Princess Charlotte's education be not only intellectually rigorous, but useful too as opposed to dedicated only to feminine pursuits. She fretted over news that the little girl was to be inoculated and perhaps remembering the fate of Alfred and Octavius, rejoiced to hear that the matter had passed without any complications.

In Royal's letters, we get a glimpse into the character of the woman who believed that people 'must be just before they are generous.' Never indulged in her own childhood, she counselled Lady Elgin against allowing her young charge to be spoiled. Perhaps Royal remembered her own tireless education when she commented that, 'I love a steady quiet way with children', for under her mother's critical and capricious gaze, this was something that she herself had never truly experienced. Yet just as the queen had kept Royal close, it seemed that this was one thing that had rubbed off as she wrote that, 'if ever the Almighty blesses me with girls, it shall be my object to have them constantly with me, and to try gently to correct little faults. A lie or the proof of a bad heart, I think, alone allows of severity.'

Royal was not a woman who one could ever accuse of having 'a bad heart'. In her letter to Lady Elgin she constantly advocates the need for gentleness, for not allowing too much vanity and for guidance rather than rigid discipline. She allowed herself too to admit that she felt a pang of envy for her siblings, who were still able to see one another while she was far, far away. As the seething conflicts in Europe settled down, Royal's nostalgia was quietened by visits from some of her siblings, but we can hardly resent her some wistfulness whenever she received reports of her young niece and the family she had left behind.

Yet if Royal had remained in England, unmarried and at the beck and call of her mother, one struggles to imagine a life that would have been fulfilling. Marriage brought with it challenges and sadness too, but it also brought the opportunity to be more than a daughter at last.

The Trouble with France

Along with his father's vast collection of books, including more than eight thousand different editions of the bible, the Duke of Württemberg had inherited a wealth of political problems. Among them was an ongoing dispute with France, which Frederick was determined to settle once and for all. Fearing that the French might be poised to invade Württemberg, he urged his wife to leave for her own safety but Royal, having fought so long for her own establishment, refused.

Frederick believed that Royal's illustrious parentage would make her a prize prisoner for France but still she resisted until in 1800 there appeared to be little choice. With French troops marching into Württemberg the electoral family and their attendants were forced to flee. They took up residence in Erlangen, whilst Frederick made desperate attempts to win support for his embattled duchy in Vienna. Here he grew frustrated, wondering why he had received no help from Britain to secure his lands against the French invasion, especially considering his marital connections. The assumed benefits of his shrewd wedding were *not* paying off.

On 10 December 1800 Royal informed her father that, 'We are now in a very unpleasant situation here, [...] the French have taken possession of Nuremberg and their troops are constantly marching through this town and are quartered in all the villages round about, which makes me an absolute prisoner, as yesterday I attempted to walk round the town and at a very small distance we saw a patrol, which prevents our going out at all as in Erlangen there is no end of the French soldiers who are to be met with constantly in the streets.'[22]

Frederick's alliance with the Holy Roman Empire against Napoleon's advance was costing him dear and there were precious few benefits to be gained by adhering to it as his duchy fell apart around him. With his efforts in Vienna exhausted, the writing was on the wall. It was time for Napoleon and Frederick to make their peace.

In England this new development was understandably frowned on, though equally it was seen as simply the natural progression, given the situation between the embattled Holy Roman Empire and the French Republic. Indeed, the Empire was at the beginning of its drawn-out death throes whilst in Württemberg, things were settling at last.

Gone was Royal's fear of what might become of her in exile at Erlangen and she was instead settled in her Ludwigsburg idyll once more, tending the gardens and the duke's prized farm. Like George and Charlotte, Frederick and Royal had a shared love of botany and agriculture. For Royal, this wasn't a matter simply of indulgence, but of income. As she wrote to her father:

'The sheep are all of the Spanish breed and the wool has been sold this year for above twelve guineas a hundredweight which appears to me dearer than it used to be in England. Much pains is taken to improve the wool as there is a very good cloth manufactory here. The troops as well as all the livery are clothed in it, and some of the cloths are so good that the Duke often wears them. In general the spirit of industry which the people exert in agriculture is very pleasant to see, and I hope the encouragement the Duke gives them will do a great deal of good. Your Majesty having taken so much to farming is very much admired abroad and looked on as one of the great causes of the improvements in England.'[23]

All of this was welcome news to King George, whose health was suffering once more. But as her father was struggling, Royal wasn't just blossoming, she was positively blooming. Perhaps unsurprisingly for the wife of a man who was famed for his immense weight, in the years following her miscarriage, Royal too began to pile on the pounds. No longer governed by the meagre and plain meals of Windsor and Kew she indulged herself just as Frederick did and the duke and duchess grew round together. After a visit to Württemberg several years later her sister, Augusta, wrote that 'she is very large and bulky. Her face is very broad and fat, which makes her features appear quite small and distended. But what strikes the most is, that from not wearing the least bit of corset, her stomach and hips are something quite extraordinary.'

In fact, what Augusta was seeing wasn't simply indulgence, but the first symptoms of the illness that would eventually claim Royal's life. Whether Frederick's reputation as an abusive spouse can be proven is debateable though. Certainly, the rumours that followed him and Napoleon's own comment that Royal's husband 'was a brute, though a man of talent [who] ill treated her' seems to suggest that we cannot dismiss the allegations out of hand, Royal herself made no such complaints. Did pride prevent her from speaking out or perhaps fear that she might be returned to the life she had escaped from? If so, we can but speculate, for the princess herself left behind no such word.

At Odds

With Württemberg's alliance with France, Duke Frederick had proven once and for all that he had given up on any hopes that his marriage might reap diplomatic dividends. The late duke had converted from

Catholicism to Protestantism in the hope of being made an elector, a rank which had always escaped him, and his conversion did nothing to change that. When Frederick gave his loyalty and the use of his armies to Napoleon, however, an electorate was the gift that followed. Though at home in Great Britain the royal family were appalled that their son-in-law had allied with France, in Württemberg, celebrations were afoot to mark the promotion of the duke and duchess to elector and electress.

Even as George grew more unwell in England, in France, Napoleon was going from strength to strength. As the nineteenth century rolled on through its early years, the newly crowned French emperor was of a mind to reward those who had been loyal and those who might, in the future, prove useful. He met Royal in person and was 'much pleased with her', no doubt much to the annoyance of her mother and father. Yet what her mother and father had to say was of little consequence now. Indeed, in 1807 Napoleon was pleased to note that Royal 'contributed materially towards effecting the marriage between [Napoleon's] brother Jerome and the Princess Catherine, daughter of [Frederick] by a former marriage.'[24] The lady of Württemberg had swiftly learned the ropes.

Just a couple of years after Württemberg became an electorate, it took the next step along the regal ranks and was proclaimed a kingdom. On 1 January 1806, the elector and electress were crowned King and Queen of Württemberg. A vast crown was erected atop of the royal palace in recognition of this new honour and Royal, once the princess who dreamed of freedom, must have wondered at her new-found position.

One person who *certainly* wondered at it was George III. He refused to address his daughter as queen of anywhere, for he didn't recognise the kingdom that Napoleon had created. That refusal to acknowledge the crowning, in addition to her husband's allegiance to Napoleon, meant that Royal was unable to visit Britain and her sisters were likewise unable to visit her, so she learned of the death of Amelia, her youngest sibling, without being able to say a final farewell in person. Her experiences of the king's progressing mental health problems were second-hand too, as she was kept at a remove from the family dramas she had left behind. It's tempting to speculate that homesickness might have been amongst the reasons for rumours of her supposed return to England in 1813, but newspapers hinted darkly at something more sinister in the intentions of the wife of the roundly distrusted and disliked Frederick. In fact, no such return to England took place. Whether a happy wife or the puppet of Napoleon, Royal stayed in her crowned palace.

> '[Arrangements had been] made, with the consent of the Court of Wirtemburg [sic], for the departure of the late PRINCESS ROYAL of ENGLAND from that country, and her future residence in her native land. It is not for us to mention the causes which have led to this extraordinary and unexpected measure, but we can vouch for the correctness of the statement. [25]

Eventually the correspondence between Royal and her family grew increasingly sporadic until, just as he had when he pledged his allegiance to Napoleon, her husband switched sides again. With the decline in the fortunes of France, Württemberg wisely chose to align itself with Russia. Frederick's sister, Sophia Dorothea, had taken the name Maria Feodorovna when she married Paul I of Russia and their son, Tsar Alexander I, now ruled Russia. Frederick was quick to capitalise on the identity of this invaluable nephew, as well as his status as son-in-law to George III as well. It was a canny move and when the Congress of Vienna met in 1814 to carve up European territory after the fall of Napoleon, Frederick was confirmed as King of Württemberg. George III was by then far too unwell to know or care but to the rest of the world it was official. Royal was inarguably a queen.

It was to be the last victory in a life that had been full of reversals and as October 1816 drew to a close, Frederick died. As he passed away his daughter-in-law gave birth to another member of the Württemberg dynasty.

One in, one out.

Dowager

A widow before her twentieth wedding anniversary, the Princess Royal mourned her husband deeply. Her brother, Prince Edward, Duke of Kent, was with her when Frederick died and though Royal must have taken comfort in the proximity of a member of her family, she grieved for her husband just the same. Royal honoured Frederick for the rest of her days and for every year that followed, she continued to mark his birthday. With her late husband succeeded as king by his son, William I, Royal now settled into life as a queen dowager. She filled her long days with art and reading and trips to take the waters for her health. She was loved by her subjects for her philanthropy and by her stepchildren for her maternal nature.

The death of Frederick was the overture to a period that would hit Royal hard. Next came news that her beloved niece, Princess Charlotte of Wales, had died whilst delivering a stillborn baby, which must have reawakened memories of her own sad loss so many years ago. This was followed by the death of Queen Charlotte, Royal's mother. By now suffering from dementia having long since handed the reins of the kingdom to his son, the Prince Regent - formerly Wales - George knew nothing of the death of his wife. Next came the death of her brother, the Duke of Kent, followed by the passing of King George III. He had never been reunited with his oldest daughter.

Royal was now the senior female member of the British royal family, though she hadn't set foot in the country for a quarter of a decade. century She lived in splendour with her family and happily received visitors, the once timid girl having flourished into a competent and welcoming hostess. Although ill health prevented her from attending the baptism ceremony, Royal served as a godmother to the future Queen Victoria at her christening in 1819, a ray of sunshine amongst the mourning. Her presence at her father's funeral was also made impossible by her failing health, but Royal was a fighter. She wasn't beaten yet.

The queen dowager of Württemberg's days were growing short, but she was determined to soldier on. Thirty years after she had sailed from Harwich, she returned to her native land seeking treatment for dropsy. Royal's ship reached Greenwich in the first week of June 1827 and amidst great ceremony, she joined her family for supper. The people turned out in their droves to cheer for their returning princess and despite her illness, Royal was buoyed by so many friendly faces. She rejoiced to finally meet her goddaughter, little Princess Victoria, and revelled in a return to the people and places that had once been her entire life. They were all older, of course, and some were gone, but those that remained were a tonic for the ailing woman.

Unsurprisingly, Royal had changed in the years that she'd been away. Lady Louisa Stuart wrote that people 'talked of [Royal's] size as something enormous, which it really is not. She is rather shapeless than fat, not having worn stays of any kind these twenty years.'[26] Still as down to earth as ever despite the splendour of her life, Royal's clothes were 'nothing extraordinary, what anybody's would be who went with their own few grey hairs instead of wearing a wig.'[27] It is, I think, nothing less than we have come to expect from the queen dowager.

For the duration of her stay in England, Royal was attended by her sister, Augusta, but her medical needs were in the hands of a team of physicians led by Sir Astley Cooper. Despite the presence of these eminent doctors the dropsy which afflicted Royal proved difficult to treat. There could be no cure, only temporary relief. She returned home in October through violent storms, telling her concerned attendants as the boat was lashed by waves, 'I am here in the hand of God as much as at home in my bed.'[28] The queen of Württemberg was preparing for her final days.

Soon after she reached Württemberg, Royal's declining health rendered her virtually immobile. She had to be carried from room to room and tried to soldier on as though nothing had changed, yet the spreading dropsy left her with terrible chest pains and mounting confusion. A year after she had returned to her marital home, she took to her bed for the final few days of her life.

Surrounded by the stepfamily who adored her, Royal died just a week after her sixty-second birthday. She was laid to rest beside her husband in the country that had come to regard her as its own beloved daughter.

Act Three

Princess Augusta Sophia of the United Kingdom (8 November 1768 – 22 September 1840)

The Second Daughter

Given the timidity of the Princess Royal, one might expect that this will be a story of contrasts, of the second daughter exhibiting the fire that the first did not. In fact, the truth was very different. Born just two years after Royal, Princess Augusta proved to be another shy child, if a shy child with a bad temper at times, as shown by her childhood letters, in which she dutifully records for posterity the moments when she misbehaved: 'this morning I behaved Pretty well and this afternoon quite well'[1]. Spared the role of secretary to Queen Charlotte, Augusta didn't stay shy for long and by the time Frances Burney met the princess in her seventeenth year she found Augusta to have 'a great deal of sport in her disposition'. This would serve Augusta well in what were sometimes challenging years.

Augusta made her debut at the age of 13 when she appeared at her father's birthday ball. She was so terrified of the spotlight that Queen Charlotte didn't mention the event to her until days before and when she did, Augusta took the news badly. So badly, in fact, that she was stunned into silence. She abhorred crowds and ceremony so to be the centre of attention was the worst thing that she could imagine. Yet like her sibling, Augusta was well-trained, and she acquitted herself admirably at her debut. Unlike Royal, she even managed to keep her shoes on her feet!

Just like her elder sister, Augusta's hopes for the future and for that gay Hanoverian court that her father envisioned as a screening place for possible bridegrooms were smashed by his illness. She and Royal were sucked into the maelstrom of anguish and became both their mother's confidantes and their father's tonic. Augusta was moved into a makeshift bed in Charlotte's bedroom and she and her sisters often shared the queen's room, forming a cabal of mother and daughters who brooded together over the fate of the king, hidden behind closed doors. Week after week, month after month passed in which the elder girls cared for their desperate mother as she in turn fretted over her chattering husband. The woman who had raised them with fortitude and stern dedication, overseeing their education, their dress, their comportment, was now scarcely able to eat. Charlotte rarely slept and paced back and forth across her apartments, waiting for the next news from the king's doctors.

> 'The Queen is almost overpowered with some secret terror. [...] To-day she gave up the conflict when I was alone with her and burst into a violent fit of tears. It was very, very terrible to see! [...] Sometimes she walks up and down the room without uttering a word, but shaking her head frequently, and in evident distress and irresolution.'[2]

Augusta was part of the travelling party that journeyed to the coast on that trip which had ignited Royal's wish for freedom and when the younger sister got a taste of the fun of the seaside, she revelled in it. She bathed in the sea and watched the ships with fascination, taking tours of naval vessels and relishing the demonstrations of British sea power. She boasted that, 'I am a famous sailor' and she wore an anchor as her symbol on her jewellery, both as an acknowledgement of her closeness to her brother, William IV, *the Sailor King*, and her own love of the sea.

One cannot help but wonder if Augusta might have followed the example of some of her brothers and taken to the waves if only propriety and gender had allowed. For young Augusta, of course, filled with enthusiasm and excitement for the open sea, there was to be no life on the ocean waves. Yet Augusta wasn't like the Princess Royal, retiring and happy to spend hours studying botany or working at her easel; she was a gifted musician who delighted in entertaining others with her talents. She loved to roam outside with her brothers, and even joined them at cricket or other games, regardless of propriety. But despite her love of sport she was a princess and whether at Weymouth or Windsor, she had to behave accordingly.

Marriage Material

Though Augusta loved every moment of the tour to the south west, all too soon it was over. She had to leave behind the sailors and the merry, welcoming parties, the dancing maidens and floral bowers that greeted the royal party at every turn and go back to the life that she had always known. Like Royal, Augusta was no longer a little girl and just as her older sister began to dream of marriage, the thought wasn't far from Augusta's mind either when the court reassembled. Of course, Royal's future had to come first, but that didn't stop courtiers from attempting a little bit of matchmaking on behalf of the younger, prettier princess.

Despite the misery endured at the Danish court by the king's sister, Caroline Matilda, the first tentative suitor came from that very country. Or rather, it might be more appropriate to say that the first tentative *interest* came from Denmark, for no young man made the trip to England to press his suit. The proposed bridegroom was Frederick, the Crown Prince of Denmark, son of the unfortunate Caroline Matilda and her former husband, Christian VII. The proposal was motivated by a sense of duty rather than any romantic interest and the king's answer was a firm *no*. On this matter George was unequivocal and with his sister's fate still fresh in his mind, he refused to even countenance a proposal from Denmark. To him, that country was one in which his daughters could expect to face nothing but misery. He would not condemn any of them to Caroline Matilda's terrible fate.

This didn't stop the matchmakers from trying. Nor did it keep Augusta from having to endure the teasing of court wags, who barracked her with jokes to which Denmark was the inevitable punchline. It tried her patience to breaking point, as the gags pointedly drew attention to one sobering fact: there was no suitor waiting in the wings. Or was there?

And so, we find ourselves once more in the company of Prince Ferdinand Frederick Augustus of Württemberg, son of Frederick II Eugene, Duke of Württemberg. Ferdinand was a celebrated and dashing soldier who was so keen to find a wife in Great Britain. Queen Charlotte found him not only amiable, but her preferred holy trinity of 'religious, modest and agreeable' which, given how she later quashed any hopes her daughters might have had for marriage, could be considered something of a minor miracle. Prince Ferdinand seemed to have it all and at a ball given to mark the end of the year, he glittered as the brightest star of all.

'He danced at Court,' remembered Charlotte Papendiek, Charlotte's wardrobe keeper and reader, who was struck by Ferdinand's 'beauty and elegant manner'[3], but a marriage to the star attraction was not on the cards for young Augusta. Not only was there the matter of Royal's unmarried state to resolve first, there was also the small issue of Ferdinand's family scandals and, to complete the hattrick, his rank. Ferdinand was not the heir to the dukedom but the fifth son, so the chances of his ever succeeding to a title of his own were scant.

Mrs Papendiek secured tickets for the queen's birthday ball, which was the next major court occasion at which she hoped to catch a glimpse of the dashing young prince. Mrs Papendiek was to be disappointed though, for in the interim George had received Ferdinand's proposal for Augusta and rejected it. Rather than dance and sparkle as he had before, this time the celebrated and dashing soldier remained in his seat towards the back of the room and refused to join the dancing. Soon afterwards, he left England, his hopes of marriage to Princess Augusta in ruins.

For a brief period, there was some agreement amongst courtiers that Prince Frederick of Orange-Nassau might be a good match for Augusta, but this lasted precisely as long as it took France to seize Holland, forcing the House of Orange to flee into exile. No princess could wed a prince without a realm, after all. It was hardly the done thing. Likewise, a proposal from Prince Frederick Adolf of Sweden, son of King Adolf Frederick, came to nothing. Even Frederick of Hesse-Homburg, eldest son of Landgrave Frederick V, found his suit dismissed. He would try again later and secure the hand of Augusta's sister, Elizabeth, instead.

If there was a man out there who would satisfy the requirements of both Charlotte and George, he had yet to make himself known. Yet with the departure of the Princess Royal for Württemberg, Princess Augusta now moved into pole position as the next daughter in line to marry. Sadly, things would not prove quite as simple as all that.

With a distinct shortage of eligible men to hand, Augusta later developed a close attachment to Sir Henry Halford, the royal physician. Though some have assumed that she became the doctor's mistress, this is only speculation. Halford and Augusta frequently exchanged long letters on the health of the king and it's possible, I think, that in these exchanges she was able to grasp at some measure of certainty in the upheaval that

George's illness caused to his family. Whether it became a romance, I am less convinced. The thing with Augusta is that one could never tell what she was really thinking behind her placid smile. As her father once noted of her, 'she looks interesting – she looks as if she knew more than she would say.'[4]

Such was the cabal of the Georgian princesses.

Meeting the General

When the Princess Royal left to start her new life, Augusta stepped into the unrewarding role of her mother's closest confidante. It was a job that nobody would envy but Augusta, cheery of disposition and usually able to look on the bright side in a way that Royal could not, was more equipped than most to deal with it. Her parents were distracted by concerns for the health of Princess Amelia, their youngest daughter, but something – or someone – else was to tear Augusta's attention away from family matters. He was to be the first of several equerries to intrigue with the royal daughters.

Among the visitors to Windsor as the eighteenth century drew to an end was Major Brent Spencer, an Anglo-Irish officer and eventually a general who had already enjoyed a long and successful career. Born in 1760, Spencer had become a commissioned officer at the age of 18 and had fought both in the American War of Independence and the War of the First Coalition. Just before his fateful meeting with Princess Augusta he had led the 40th Regiment of Foot in Holland and his career would continue apace, celebrated at every turn. He eventually fell from grace with the Duke of Wellington, who called him 'a very puzzle-headed fellow', and was relieved of his command in 1811, but this simply left him free to pursue a new career as the honourable Member for Sligo, a constituency he came to represent in 1815.

According to one of the men who had served under his command, Spencer was 'a zealous, gallant officer, without any great military genius; anxious and fidgety when there was nothing to do, but, once under fire, looking like a philosopher solving a problem, perfectly cool and self-possessed'[5]. Put simply he was not the sort of man who would flourish with little to do.

Augusta, who once wrote to the Prince of Wales that, 'I have just seen the Blues. I broke part of the last commandment immediately'[6], was smitten by the dashing officer. Though she might have claimed that her enthusiasm for the Blues was simply because Wales dreamed of commanding them, ever since those thrilling days mixing with the officers of the navy on the trip to Weymouth, she had dreamed of a uniformed fellow to squire her. In a letter to Wales she wrote breathlessly, 'I intend for the rest of my life to be very despotic till I have a lord and master'[7], and in Spencer, she was sure she had found him.

Yet Spencer wasn't only far, far below her rank, he was also betrothed to Frances Canning (the sister of his brother-in-law), an engagement that was mysteriously called off not long after he first made the acquaintance of Princess Augusta. Surely the princess couldn't possibly have believed that one day her father would permit her to become the wife of this officer, no matter how celebrated and dashing he might be? The king had denied the suits of princes and even the heir to a kingdom. He would not climb down for a soldier, regardless of how much his daughter adored him.

On a personal level, the king liked Spencer and even appointed him as an equerry. Now at least Spencer was nearby, if still unobtainable, and at some point, it seems that he and Augusta became lovers when she was in her early thirties. She called him 'the secret of her heart' and she knew that there could be no marriage between them, but it didn't stop her from hoping. Augusta was a true romantic as suggested by the fact that she had once penned a letter to her brother, Wales, in which she urged him to make his affair with Maria Fitzherbert public. Though already unhappily married and estranged from Caroline of Brunswick, Amelia honestly believed that true love might still conquer all for him.

Perhaps she believed it for herself too.

A Doughty Mother

In their cloistered life, the daughters of George and Charlotte grew more melancholy as their horizons shrank far from Weymouth and Devon, dictated by their father's madness and their mother's need to control at least some aspect of her world. They were obliged to remain at Windsor or Kew, and to be tormented by the sound of the king ranting, his hysterical laughter waking them from sleep or ringing through the palace, uncanny in the stillness. When Charlotte married George, he had become her whole life and in the midst of their vast family, she had sought to create the perfect royal household, filled with upstanding princes and obedient princesses. Yet if her sons had insisted – quite legitimately - on becoming independent, she could at least prevent her daughters from following their example. She would keep them clutching at her skirts, providing her with the companionship her husband could not.

At first Charlotte had been the very model of a queen, the quintessential mother, wife and hostess, disinterested in political game playing and devoted to hearth and husband. There were to be no royal mistresses to sully the marriage of George III, nor any scandal whispered about his unimpeachable wife. When the king's illness took hold of him though, Charlotte found herself as a queen without a king, a hostess without anybody to host, and in 1811, the embers of political and constitutional change finally burst into flame.

> 'Rumour says, that the Physicians all concurred in their expectations of the KING's recovery; but they thought it improbable that he could be capable of returning to business for a considerable time to come. They did not perfectly agree as to the precise time, but the result of their report, we understand to be, that the Regency must take place.'[8]

There had been talk of a Regency before, but it had come to nothing. The death of Princess Amelia in 1810, however, finally tipped the balance and plunged the king into a new phase of insanity from which he would never recover. This time there could be no turning back from the brink.

On 5 February 1811, the Prince of Wales was appointed Prince Regent and Queen Charlotte was compelled to face the sad truth that the husband she had known and loved was gone forever. She drew her daughters closer than ever and their small, isolated cabal became the most exclusive female club in England. It was one to which nobody would want to belong.

Each of the unmarried girls was awarded a pension to provide for her amounting to approximately £7,900, enough for a comfortable existence. Princess Augusta, mysteriously, was given one additional farthing that her sisters did not receive. Throughout her life, the pious Augusta cared little for luxury and her new allowance didn't change that. Instead she focussed her interests on faith and charity, which endeared her to the people of Britain as much as her steadfast loyalty and unstinting care for her father did likewise. 'Her benevolence has been extended to all around,' wrote one commentator, 'her left hand knew not what her right gave away; and never was her charity marred by ostentation on the part of the giver.'[9] It was one thing to do good, but it was quite another to shout about it.

The newly enthroned Prince Regent had always cared deeply for his sisters and now he petitioned his mother to give them a little freedom, if only so they could serve as chaperones to his own growing daughter. Charlotte wouldn't hear of it. The sisters added their own voices to his request and wrote to the queen to ask for a loosening of their metaphorical stays, begging to be allowed some space to breathe after decades in the shadows. To say that Charlotte was furious doesn't do justice to the anger and resentment with which she received the request.

'[The princesses must] take a mothers [sic] advice. Let me beseech you well to Consider that your situation is very different to that of your Brothers, who by their Situations in life must appear in Public, and have their Duties to perform in which they would injure themselves if they were not to appear. But in your Sex, and under the present Melancholy Situation of your father the going to Public Amusements except where Duty calls you would be the highest mark of indecency possible. [With] every step any one of you intends to take, always to keep in remembrance that no age whatever is excepted from being criticized, and that the higher the character, the more will it be traduced.'[10]

The queen dismissed out of hand not only the possibility of her daughters making decisions for themselves, but also warned them that their now advancing ages did not make them immune from criticism regarding their morals, or perceived lack of them. They were not to attend any amusements nor be present in any house with an unmarried man unless there was another lady present, including the homes of their own brothers. Charlotte then turned on the self-pity, which was one of her particular talents and, as an apparent martyr to her thoughtless daughters, told them that she would not be able to see them for a little while as she had never 'felt as shattered in my life as I did by reading your letter. The stroke is given, and nothing can mend it.'[11] In other words, the queen intended to make her daughters suffer. What better way than withdrawing into isolation to lick her wounds?

Thanks, mum.

Filled with longing and the spirit of battle that had seen her brothers forge their own ways in the world, Augusta must have wanted to scream. She was no longer a girl, but her mother refused to acknowledge it, as if the act of denying her womanhood could make it all go away. All Augusta could do was rail in letters to the Regent that, 'we have neither Health or Spirits to support for any length of time the life which We have led for the last two years, and more Especially the Treatment which we have experienced whenever any Proposal has been made for Our absenting Ourselves for a few days from the Queen's Roof.'[12] Things had reached a head and the princesses were ready to escape Charlotte's miserable world and strike out on their own.

Yet the Prince Regent, the man who held a country in his hand, was the only one of Charlotte's children who was able to bend her to his will and even then, it had to be a delicate operation. It took some time and more than a few tears but eventually the queen acquiesced a little and the princess' threats of leaving were quelled. The princesses must still be companions to her and the king at Windsor, she decided, but contrary to her earlier assertions she would permit them to move about in society a little. And only a little.

But for the princesses who had been so long imprisoned, a little was all they needed.

The Secret Heart

As the decade wore on, Princess Augusta's passion for Brent Spencer never wavered and unlike some of her siblings' relationships, her liaison did not become the subject of idle court gossip either. Instead, the couple was discrete and Augusta alone was left to fret and worry about her lover's fate when Spencer was serving overseas. She could at least express some of her concern as though it was for her brothers who served, but secretly she waited for news that Brent Spencer would be safely delivered to her once more.

In 1808 Augusta confided her secret passion to the Prince of Wales, who gently admitted that her confession was less of a surprise than she might have expected it to be. Though self-obsessed and extravagant, sometimes to the point of comedy, Wales was always fond of his sisters and even if he hadn't guessed who the object of her worry was, he had noticed Augusta's anxious countenance and wondered at the reason for it. Now at last her secret could be told and though unburdening herself could do nothing to help her hopeless situation, Augusta had at least been able to share the reason for her occasional dejection. It must have been an immense relief.

As an equerry to the king, Brent Spencer frequently came into the same company as Augusta in his official capacity. In a case of so near and yet so far, both found these meetings difficult and Spencer offered to resign his position at court in order to save Augusta the agony of being able to see him without being able to be with him, as it were, but she refused to even countenance such an idea. Instead the princess urged him to retain his position as equerry and promised to make every effort not to 'express my feelings both for his sake and my own.'

In confessing to her attachment, Augusta also recognised that the time might come when Spencer went abroad in the service of his country and did not return to her arms. Should this happen, at least Augusta now knew that Wales would lend her his shoulder in consolation, for she could hardly share her grief with anyone else.

Poor Puss, as Wales termed Augusta, was besotted with her soldier. By now in her forties and still unmarried, she longed to make matters official. When Wales, who had always been her champion, became Regent, that possibility came within her grasp for the first time.

Augusta admitted to her brother that she and Spencer had pledged themselves to one another almost a decade earlier and now they wanted to make it official. She sensibly acknowledged that such an arrangement couldn't be made public, but that didn't matter to the couple. What mattered was that she and Spencer could finally and truthfully be together, both in the eyes of the law and the Lord. She wrote to the Prince Regent in heartbreakingly honest terms, begging for his help.

'I now beseech you, my Dearest, to consider our *situation*.
If it is in your power to make us happy I know you will.
I am sensible that should you agree to our Union it can

only proceed from your affection for me, and your desire of promoting my happiness and that of a Worthy Man. It is not a fancy taken up vaguely, our acquaintance having existed for twelve years, and our attachment been *mutually acknowledged nine years ago.* To you we look up, for our future comfort and peace of mind. Your sanction is what we aspire to! And as of course it will be necessary to keep it a Secret, and as it must be quite a Private Marriage, if you think it more proper in your Situation not to be present at it (which I need not assure you would be a sad disappointment to us both) I entreat your permission that dear Frederick may attend for you. The world, if it ever hears of this Circumstance, may be astonished, but it cannot blame our conduct, especially when it knows we are supported and encouraged by my Brothers, nor can it allege any deceit to our behaviour. Our Sentiments were of too delicate a Nature for us to make them known, unless at a moment when we might hope to have our sufferings relieved. Nothing is more repugnant to my Principles or more grating to my feelings than not acting with Candour to every individual; and particularly so towards my *own* family, but this was my own Secret, and in no particular can I tax my heart with having deceived them on this occasion, for there is no duplicity in Silence.'[13]

So far, so good and as a man who had made an illegal marriage of his own and knew more than a thing or two about matters of the heart, we must imagine that the prince was broadly sympathetic. How though would he react to the real nub of the matter and the fact that he might be Regent with power over a country, but he still had a fierce and dominant mother residing at home?

'Should your Answer be favourable to my Heart's Dearest and nearest wish, I shall beg of you to have the goodness to name it to the Queen. No consideration in the world (even certain of all that is *essential, Your Permission*) shall make me take such a step unknown to Her. I owe it to Her as my Mother, though I am too honest to affect asking for *Her consent, as it is not necessary*. Nor shall the most Anxious wish of my Heart ever make me unjust or unreasonable. I am certain the Queen cannot approve if She merely thinks of my birth and station. But that is the *only reason* She can object to it, and I shall never blame Her for it. But when she considers the Character of the Man, the faithfulness and length of our attachment, and the struggles that I have been compelled to make, never retracting from any of my Duties, though suffering Martyrdom from anxiety of *Mind* and *deprivation of happiness*, I am sure that She will say long and great has been my trial, and correct has been my Conduct.'[14]

Well, a girl can dream, can't she?

'These, my Beloved Brother, are the Genuine Sentiments of my Heart. I have nothing to disguise upon the subject, having once named it to You, but I will confess that I am proud of possessing the Affection and good opinion of an Honest Man and highly distinguished Character, and I am sure that what You can do to make us happy You will not leave undone.'[15]

In begging the Regent to make her case to the queen, Augusta was a hopeful if guarded girl once more, afraid of her mother and desperate to win her approval. Such approval would never be forthcoming from Charlotte who, regardless of the challenges she had faced in the years of her marriage, believed in rank above all else. She would never give a match between one of her daughters and a soldier her blessing, regardless of how celebrated he might be, and Augusta knew her mother well enough to realise this. Though she had confided in the Regent and, we might assume since she names him as a possible attendee at her longed-for wedding, also the Duke of York, Augusta's parents remained ignorant of her attachment.

By the time Augusta penned her letter to the Regent, Spencer's military career was over. He had survived against the odds and come home to her once and for all, never to be put in danger in the name of King and country again.

But did the Regent grant her wish and permit a secret marriage for his sister? Simply put, we don't know, but I believe that the answer is *probably*. Augusta and the Prince Regent were devoted siblings, his *Poor Puss* a constant correspondent with her brother even when he was at odds with his parents. He knew better than anyone how the girls were cloistered by Charlotte and he knew the agony of being kept from the one you love. Though his illegal marriage to Maria Fitzherbert ended unhappily and his official marriage to Caroline of Brunswick was an infamous disaster, the Regent nursed a passion for Mrs Fitzherbert to his dying day. Indeed, when he was laid to rest many years later, it was with her miniature around his corpulent neck.

The Regent was a romantic, a dreamer, and he had no truck with his mother's efforts to keep her girls at home. With a list of lovers from every social station stretching right back to his coming of age, the love between a princess and a soldier would not be so unthinkable as all that. Besides, even if there was no marriage as such, the relationship between Augusta and Spencer was one of the most enduring amongst the children of Charlotte and George. As such it hardly needed a legal seal to make it real, though Augusta would no doubt have wished for one. She was a princess, after all.

Spencer was recognised as someone to be admired by the royal family. He was installed as a Knight of the Bath in 1812 by the Duke of York and who should be there to watch the investiture ceremony but Princess Augusta? He progressed through the order at a rapid rate and was one of the knights chosen to attend the Coronation of George IV, the very man who Augusta had petitioned for permission to marry. Of perhaps even more note is the fact that when Princess Charlotte of Wales died in 1817, Spencer was the man selected to carry news of her death to Windsor on behalf of the home secretary and former prime minister, Viscount Sidmouth. This is all highly circumstantial, of course, but it is also significant. No longer a serving officer or an equerry to the king, Brent Spencer was still entrusted with this most important and sensitive duty.

And to whose door did he deliver this unhappy news? Who, but Princess Augusta?

> '[Spencer] came to my door, and His step was so heavy; & his knock *so short*, it was really like the Knell of Death. But

when I saw His face, I called out, "Oh! that look kills me."
We could neither of us speak a Word; but after a little while
He put Lord Sidmouth's most distressing but humane letter
into my trembling hand: & God knows what my feelings
were *and are.*'[16]

At least Augusta had Brent Spencer with her as that terrible announcement
sank in.

An Establishment

As Queen Charlotte grew older and her surviving daughters settled
into middle age the king languished at Windsor, insensible and unable
to recognise his own family. Augusta made her home at the castle
too, never far from the father she adored. Of her letter begging for
permission to marry no more was said but Spencer was a constant
presence at Windsor, respectable and attentive as duty demanded.
The couple made occasional and innocent forays out into the public
eye such as when 'Princess Augusta rode on horseback, attended by
Sir Brent Spencer,'[17] but there was no scandal to be harvested from
such outings. They were just everyday events in a royal household
dominated by the king's illness. Despite her father's suffering, Princess
Augusta's life progressed much as it always had, her role stuck halfway
between nurse and princess. She played hostess to friends including
that old retainer, Frances Burney, making up melodies and singing
along tunefully at the piano keyboard for the pleasure of her guests,
ever cheery, never changing.

At home in Württemberg meanwhile, the Princess Royal received
word of her mother's failing health and began to reflect on what this
all might mean to her unmarried sisters. She apparently knew nothing
of Augusta's attachment to her muddled military man and wrote that
'from her great shyness, [Augusta] stands more in need of a real, steady
friend than the rest of her Sisters.'[18] Unaware of Brent Spencer's place
in Augusta's heart she hoped that the Regent would provide Augusta
and Sophia with 'separate establishments; as, though both amiable,
their dispositions and tastes are too different for them to be perfectly
comfortable if they were to live together.'[19]

Augusta was left bereft at the loss of her mother and she was with other members of her family at Queen Charlotte's side when she died. Together Augusta and Mary had nursed the frail woman in her dying days, a constant presence at her bedside whether day or night, ready to meet her every need. In the immediate aftermath of the queen's death, Princess Mary told Lady Harcourt that 'poor Augusta was really overwhelmed at first, but a walk afterwards calmed and composed her.'[20] All that would heal her grief, however, was time.

The doughty Queen Charlotte was not an easy woman to get along with but after decades spent as her companions it's hardly surprising that the royal daughters pined for her. She had filled their days in childhood and adulthood and her absence left a gaping hole in their lives which echoed with silence. Yet perhaps the loss of the king was less tumultuous, for he had long since ceased to be recognisable as the loving and playful parent who had visited the royal nursery and revelled in the company of the children. Instead he was a blind shadow of that man, barking orders at invisible soldiers and chatting to the ghosts of his dead children.

Augusta's family seemed to be falling like flies. After the sadness of losing Princess Charlotte followed by the queen, the next death to afflict the royal household was that of Edward, Duke of Kent, who passed away just nine days before the king, leaving Augusta devastated, and his only child, the future Queen Victoria, fatherless. Augusta was doing her best to manage the care of the king when she received word that her brother was sickening, having caught a cold after refusing to change out of his wet boots following an outing in bad weather. The cold progressed and Edward's worried wife summoned the physician to the king, Sir David Dundas, to come and tend the ailing duke. Dundas asked Augusta which patient took precedence – monarch or duke - and she took it upon herself to write to the duchess and tell her that Sir David was otherwise engaged caring for the king. Instead another physician would be sent to treat the ailing Kent.

Dundas suggested the late queen's former physician, Dr Maton, who rushed to the Duke of Kent's side to administer care. Sadly, 'notwithstanding repeated blisters, bleedings, Cuppings, and Leeches, the fever and Inflammation returned every night at the same hour'. That same fever and inflammation killed the duke within days. Augusta lamented how well Kent had been just a few weeks earlier when she'd seen him on his way to Sidmouth. Now, for the want of fresh, dry boots, he was dead.

Augusta had barely had time to process her brother's death when her father finally breathed his last. After so many years caring for him and Queen Charlotte, Princess Mary noted that 'Augusta is much more composed than after the poor Q's death', which is hardly surprising. Augusta had watched the king suffer and weaken, watched him grow blind, immobile and insensible, and she had suffered alongside him. She was due a change of air.

In fact, the establishment Royal had reflected on is precisely what Augusta received following the death of Queen Charlotte, who bequeathed Frogmore to her in her will. Though Augusta remained at Windsor whilst the king lived, upon his death, she hastened to Frogmore, ready to fill her days with the flora and fauna that would become her passion as she entered the last decades of her life. Here she took up residence in the Augusta Tower, her new apartment situated directly beneath the chambers that had once belonged to her mother. Perhaps it was a matter of respect or maybe she felt that the air of martyred disapproval pervaded those rooms still, but whatever the reason Augusta made no effort to occupy them. Nothing could be more perfect than Frogmore, for who should be her near neighbour there but Brent Spencer?

Royal and Augusta were reunited soon after the death of the king when the latter visited Württemberg and though Augusta must have missed Spencer during her trip, no doubt the longed-for reunion with her sibling was a tonic to the sisters after the death of both their mother and father. Augusta also took the opportunity to visit another sister, Elizabeth, who had married in 1818 to become Landgravine of Hesse-Homburg, proving once and for all that the sisters might have been held back, but never lost their longing for escape. All they needed was opportunity.

Augusta rejoiced in seeing how happy Royal had become in her adopted land and when her elder sister visited England just prior to her death, she and Augusta passed many long and happy hours together. Augusta wrote approvingly that Royal 'had a very delightfull [sic] Society, both of Ladies and Gentlemen,' and related at length her sister's daily routine of family visits and socialising. She was delighted to be received by Royal's stepfamily with all the warmth of blood relations and commented that 'I was quite the aunt' of the queen dowager's granddaughters. Augusta, of course, had no children of her own and never would, but in the company of her sibling she could rejoice in the easy joy of childish company once more, safe in the knowledge that her soldier was waiting for her at home.

With her beloved brother now both king and widower following the death of his loathed and estranged wife, Augusta became his hostess in society. However, whenever the newly enthroned king was attended by his mistress, Lady Conyngham, Augusta refused to be present. When her brother asked why she insisted on what he regarded to be empty gestures of propriety, she told him, 'If you command my attendance as *King*, I will obey you; but if you ask me as a *brother* to come, nothing will induce me.'[21]

He didn't ask again.

Widowhood

> 'Died. Suddenly, General Sir Brent Spencer. Bart. K.C.B. &c. of the Lee, near Great Missenden, Bucks.[22]

Brent Spencer died at the age of 68 at the close of 1828, after a quarter of a century as the partner and, perhaps, husband of Princess Augusta. More than 150 years later, a miniature of Princess Augusta came up for auction. It was alleged to have been removed from Spencer's neck before burial and was inscribed with the letters *AS*, for Augusta Sophia.

Or, of course, Augusta Spencer.

Just as we can't know if Spencer ever married Augusta, so too are we in the dark regarding the state of their relationship at the time of his death and unsurprisingly, Augusta made no mention of her loss. Instead she continued to live her quiet life, making visits to friends and family and spending some time in Brighton to benefit from the sea air. Even as Augusta's health grew troublesome, she never failed to welcome visitors with her usual good cheer and happy countenance but eventually it became more and more difficult for her to walk in the gardens she loved. When William IV died in 1837 and his wife, Adelaide, moved out of Clarence House, Augusta took up residence there instead. She was to remain in her new home for the final three years of her life. She was also to become a close and valued confidante of the newly widowed Queen Dowager Adelaide, who was as devoted to her sister-in-law as she was to any blood relative.

With the death of her sister, Elizabeth, in 1840, Augusta was left bereft. She was all too aware of the encroaching years, as well as her own weakening health. When sea cures and leeches could do no more for her, she took to her bed at Clarence House, tended in her final days by the finest royal physicians. Green Park was closed to ensure that Augusta could rest in peace and the populace who had grown to love her waited to hear the sad but inevitable news of her passing. The press reported each twist and turn as she was' reduced to a very distressing state, [...] almost exhausted with pain and suffering"[23] and few held out any hope for her recovery.

Augusta was tended day and night for an intestinal obstruction and laboured in intense pain from which she could find little respite. Her niece, Queen Victoria, tracked the suffering of her beloved aunt in her journals and though she rejoiced to hear news of the older woman rallying just days before her death, all knew that there was little hope for the 71-year-old princess. Languishing in her sickbed, Augusta told Adelaide that she hoped to live long enough to see the birth of Victoria and Albert's first child. Sadly, she was to miss that happy occasion by a matter of weeks.

Princess Augusta spent her last days slipping in and out of consciousness as her life slowly ebbed away. She died on 22 September 1840 in her bed at Clarence House. At her side was her friend, Queen Dowager Adelaide, who held Augusta's hand as she drew her last breath. Though the event was a melancholy one Queen Victoria and the princess' doctors took some comfort in the fact that, for Augusta, the suffering she had endured was finally over.

> 'The Princess Augusta expired at 17 minutes past 9 o'clock last night, at Clarence House, St. James's after a long and very trying illness, which her Royal Highness bore with the utmost patience and meekness.
>
> Throughout the progress of her painful malady [...] her Royal Highness constantly maintained that amiability of temper which always characterised her.'[24]

So it was that the life of Augusta, who had known three kings and a queen, drew to an end. After lying in state at Frogmore, the first home that was truly her own, she was laid to rest at Windsor. This genial, smart, well-loved woman lived a quiet life and 'died poor – the result of a life so nobly spent'[25], but in the end, it was a happy existence. Sadly, we might never know exactly what the nature of her relationship with Brent Spencer was but even without that final piece to the puzzle, she remains an exemplary princess and one who would, I think, have flourished in her youth had she just been given the chance. She wasn't the only one.

1. Charlotte, Princess Royal.

2. Princess Augusta.

3. Princess Elizabeth.

4. Princess Mary.

5. Princess Sophia.

6. HRH Princess Amelia by Andrew
Robertson.

Above: 7. King George III and family by Richard Earlom, after Johann Zoffany, 1871.

Left: 8. King George III in old age by Samuel William Reynolds, 1820.

9. Her Most Gracious Majesty, Queen Charlotte.

10. The Prince of Wales.

11. Brent Spencer

12. Ernest Augustus, Duke of
Cumberland.

Right: 13. Her
Royal Highness the
Princess Royal by
Peltro W Tomkins,
after Johann
Heinrich Ramberg,
1801.

Below: 14. The
Coffin of Her Royal
Highness, Princess
Amelia.

Her ROYAL HIGHNESS the PRINCESS ROYAL.

Dedicated by Permission

To Her most GRACIOUS Majesty the QUEEN of Great Britain

By her Majesty's most devoted and most dutiful Subject and Servant

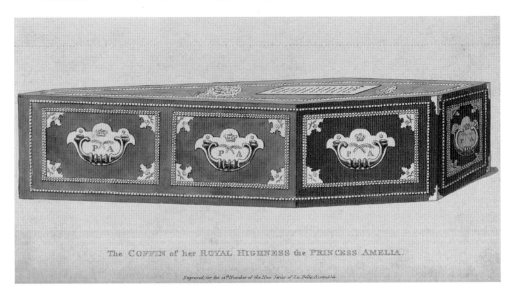

The COFFIN of her ROYAL HIGHNESS the PRINCESS AMELIA.

Engraved for the 12th Number of the New Series of La Belle Assemblee.

Left: 15. General the Honourable Charles FitzRoy.

Below: 16. Charlotte, Queen of Great Britain, and the Princess Royal by Valentine Green, after Benjamin West.

CHARLOTTE, QUEEN of GREAT BRITAIN, and the PRINCESS ROYAL.

17. King George III giving money to a woman near Weymouth by Robert Pollard, 1820.

18. Queen Charlotte holding the baby Princess Charlotte, after Francis Cotes.

19. HRH Princess Amelia.

Her ROYAL HIGHNESS the PRINCESS ELIZABETH.

20. HRH the Princess Elizabeth
by William Ward, after Johann
Heinrich Ramberg, 1801.

21. HRH Princess Sophia.

22. HRH Princess Elizabeth by Sir William Beechey.

23. Her Royal Highness Princess Augusta by Sir William Beechey, 1806.

24. Frances Burney by Charles Turner, 1840.

25. The Apotheosis of Princes
Octavius and Alfred by Sir Robert
Strange, after Benjamin West, 1787.

26. HRH Princess Elizabeth.

Left: 27. HRH Princess Mary

Below: 28. The royal family of England in the year 1787 by Thomas Stothard, 1800.

THE ROYAL FAMILY OF ENGLAND IN THE YEAR 1787.

29. Royal Beneficence by Charles Howard Hodges, after Thomas Stothard, 1793.

30. The Hombourg Waltz, showing Elizabeth and the Prince of Hesse-Homburg by
G Humphrey.

Above: 31. Caricature of the Introduction of the Duke of Württemberg (afterwards King Frederick I) to George III and Queen Charlotte previous to his marriage with Charlotte, Princess Royal of England, by Anthony Pasquin.

Left: 32. Lady Charlotte Finch by John Faber the Younger, after John Robinson.

Act Four

Princess Elizabeth of the
United Kingdom
(22 May 1770 – 10 January 1840)

Fatima

The birth of Princess Elizabeth completed the first trio of daughters and by the time she came along, the household routine was very much established. Just as George and Charlotte intended, her childhood was unremarkable and just as Royal was a talented artist and Augusta a skilled musician, Elizabeth found artistic expression through illustration. She learned her art by copying the botanical illustrations of Mary Delany, a great favourite of the king and queen, who patronised her work, and a lady the elder three princesses felt enormous affection for[1]. In the years to come, Elizabeth would use her talent for illustration to benefit her favourite charities, producing books of illustration and donating the profits from their sale.

Elizabeth didn't confine her illustrations to the page either. She produced ornamental paintings on the walls at Frogmore where she could let her inner artist run wild. For her sister, the Princess Royal, Elizabeth transformed her closet with paintings in the Japanese style, which perfectly complemented Royal's own artistic embellishments in her chambers. Elizabeth had an eye for composition and for matching the subject and style of her art to the place where it was going to be displayed. She was, in short, a prodigious talent.

The talented Elizabeth was known to her siblings as *Fatima*. Sadly, this had less to do with her artistic skills and more to do with her healthy appetite. As Mrs Papendiek wrote, 'she was born fat, and through every illness, of which she had many, she never lost flesh'[2]. In fact, Elizabeth was always what we might call *robust*, regardless of how sickly she became.

As we shall see, that was very sickly indeed.

Though her siblings might like to comment on her size, Elizabeth was also known for the sweetness of her temper. She lacked Augusta's fiery side and even drank water flavoured with sugar in the belief that it would keep her nature as calm and sweet as it had always been. It certainly kept her from fitting into her undergarments and on one occasion, when she was in her late teens, the queen had Elizabeth try on a pair of new stays in front of Mary Delany.

When the queen saw her daughter in the stays, she declared that they were too tight, and a bigger pair must be ordered. Elizabeth, no doubt dying of embarrassment, objected that they were perfectly comfortable but Charlotte, never one to allow her daughters to have their own opinions on anything, summoned Mrs Delany to have the casting vote. The blushing woman said 'her RH [Elizabeth] must be the best judge if they did not hurt her, and thus ended the business'[3]. What a mortifying moment for a young woman, to be paraded in her underwear before a friend who she both admired and respected as though she was a head of prized cattle at market. What a mortifying moment too for Mrs Delany, forced to make a declaration on such a sensitive and personal matter by the queen, no less!

Elizabeth's sprightly nature comes through vividly in the letters she wrote during her youth and perhaps never more so than in a note she sent to Lady Harcourt when travelling home from a trip to Weymouth, where she had been instrumental in organising a ball in honour of her father. She was a born organiser.

> '[I never ate] anything so disgusting as the breakfast at Woodgate's Inn, on the way from Weymouth, I thank God I never saw before and never wish to see again – bad butter, Tea, Coffee, bread, &c.; nothing to touch but boil'd eggs which were so hard that I could not eat them. So, I returned to the carriage just as I got out – starved. However, having wisely followed Sir Francis Wronghead's ways, and had a large Plumb [sic] Cake put up as *Stowage for the Stomach*, I rejoiced much at the thought of seizing this when I got back to my Coach; but the moment I had prepared myself in Battle array, with a knife in my hand to begin the massacre, they

told me it was for Mama, and my knife returned innocent to my Pocket. As I was not allowed to eat, I determined, like a true woman, to talk.'[4]

Yet even the vivacious Elizabeth could be laid low and just after New Year in 1786, only a few short years after the deaths of Alfred and Octavius, Princess Elizabeth fell mysteriously but seriously ill. As the royal family gathered at Windsor to see in the New Year, Elizabeth developed a scrofulous abscess on her side. It was caused by an infection in the lymph nodes and sent her to bed for many weeks. She had begun to show symptoms in late 1785 and in one forty-eight hour period was bled five times, but still her condition deteriorated. Despite Elizabeth's increasing frailty, physicians led by Sir George Baker continued their bloody regime. Frances Burney recorded in her diaries that not only did all the younger royal children have whooping cough, but that Elizabeth was still being bled and blistered until even *her* sweet nature was tried. Sometimes she was bled as much as a dozen times in the space of just two weeks. It was exhausting and relentless.

With the deaths of her brothers still vivid in the memory of her family, the princess languished, seeming to grow weaker by the day. Always sunny in disposition, even the cheerful Elizabeth found her illness trying and her smile faltered, with Mrs Papendiek sure that her tears were proof, if proof were needed, that the young princess was truly suffering.

Happily, Princess Elizabeth's health began to slowly recover though she remained subject to frequent and unexplained spasms for months. By the summer of 1786, she was once again mixing with her sisters and the ladies at court, including a moment of silliness recalled by Frances Burney in which the princesses made their feelings about snuff painfully clear.

'[The king] turned round from the door, and first spoke to me, with a good-humoured laugh, saying, "Miss Burney, I hear you cook snuff very well!"

"Cook snuff!" repeated the Princess Augusta, laughing, and coming up to me the moment they left the room. "Pray, Miss Burney, let me have one pinch!"

The Princess Elizabeth ran up to me, also, exclaiming, "Miss Burney, I hope you hate snuff? I hope you do, for I hate it of all things in the world!"[5]

It isn't a particularly world-shattering moment in the history of royalty, but it demonstrates the close-knit atmosphere of the court and the family under the reign of George III. His children were very much part of his life, unlike those Georges who had gone before him, each austere, distant and estranged from their sons. George III wanted to be a family man and he had fifteen children to help him fulfil his dream.

Free of snuff, Elizabeth spent much of the following two years convalescing at Windsor and was rarely seen by outsiders. She was tended to by royal physicians, who prescribed a perhaps unexpected programme of treatment that included plenty of horse-riding. So far you may be thinking that none of this sounds particularly unusual. Yet there are those who believe that Princess Elizabeth's mysterious illness, suspiciously sudden recovery and disappearance from the social scene were symptomatic of something other than ill health. In fact, in the years that have passed since she lived, there has been enduring gossip that the then then 18-year-old Princess Elizabeth was in fact with child.

A Royal Baby?

Before we delve into one of the oddest rumours to attach itself to the daughters of George III and Charlotte of Mecklenburg-Strelitz, it's important to point out that like so much rumour, this is a matter of hearsay, whispers and the odd tantalising historical aside. It first came to light as a very literal footnote by William Childe-Pemberton, who recorded in his biography of the short-lived Princess Amelia that, 'in her early youth [Elizabeth] had made a secret marriage with a Mr Ramus, by whom she had children. But the circumstances were unromantic.'[6]

Not only pregnant, but married too?

Surely that might have been a book in itself!

Yet as far as Mr Childe-Pemberton was concerned, that was that and there was nothing more to say on the matter. The omission of any further detail might seem odd, especially given that Childe-Pemberton's biography of Amelia delves in great detail into *her* heartbreak whilst remaining tight-lipped on anything further that might relate to the rumours around Elizabeth. The rumours, however, have refused to die down and though other historians and biographers have attempted to either prove or disprove them once and for all, they have been unable to do so. Perhaps the marriage registers that were kept safely in Kew Church might have been helpful in tracing a possible wedding between the rumoured royal mother and commoner father, if the registers that covered 1783 to 1845 hadn't been mysteriously spirited away at some point over the years.

No help there then, but for those who like a conspiracy this is all fuel to the fire.

Perhaps the key to the mystery lies in the identity of the supposed husband and father, the mysterious Mr Ramus of the footnote. It isn't easy to find even the tiniest grains of truth in the rumour of Elizabeth and Ramus and reports that he was a page to George III are muddy and confused. So too are reports that George III knew of and even attended a secret wedding - a preposterous allegation given the tight rein he and Charlotte kept on the marital situations of their daughters. The thought of him being present at a wedding between a princess and a page is the stuff of romantic fiction, not eighteenth century court fact.

Yet let us at least consider the prospect of Elizabeth secretly having a child, if not a wedding. A child without a confirmed father, of course, but a child, nevertheless. In the fifth volume of Crisp and Howard's *Visitation of England*, which traces the genealogical and heraldic history of the British Isles, they even give that child a name. According to the authors, Elizabeth gave birth to a daughter named Eliza, who later married a man named James Money. The couple, they claim, had a daughter together of their own and named her Marian Martha Money. If that had been true, it would have made Marian the granddaughter of Princess Elizabeth and the great-grandchild of King George III. Eliza was supposedly spirited off to India by her uncle and lived a long and happy life before returning to London many years later.

Yet Crisp and Howard didn't stop at naming the daughter of the princess. They were confident enough to declare that Eliza's father was a page to George III named George Ramus. As early as 1808, a caricature was published in which the Duke of York says goodbye to his sister with the exclamation, 'Ramus's is yours,' an allusion to the rumours of a romance. This caricature, held in the archive of the British Museum at the time of writing, is unmistakably a reference to the supposed scandal but it shouldn't be taken as evidence of a real marriage or a child. After all, as we've already seen and will see again that romance between the royal daughters and members of the household wasn't unheard of.

Perhaps there was a flirtation or a mild intrigue, but whatever it was, it sparked a certain fire in the imagination of those who liked to spread tall tales.

But there are holes in this story wide enough to drive a coach and four through. No George Ramus was employed as a page to George III unless a concerted effort has been made to scratch his very existence from history, which seems unlikely. Likewise, depending on which version of the story you choose to believe, Ramus was either a man of impeccable conduct or someone who was dismissed by the king for dishonest behaviour. Or perhaps, just maybe, there was no secret husband named Ramus at all. So, what are the facts we *do* know?

Intriguingly, there *was* a Ramus on the royal staff at the time of the supposed marriage and affair, but his name was William, or Billy. Despite having a previously unblemished record, William was dismissed by George III in 1789 after he made light of the king's illness, cruelly mocking him and his suffering. With him went several other loyal pages, all to be replaced by new appointees who were previously members of Dr Willis' household. Dr Willis was moulding the king's circle to his liking.

We might argue that this gives William Ramus motive for smearing the name of one of the king's daughters. Indeed, if we were willing to be fanciful, perhaps we might imagine that Elizabeth played some role in the king hearing of Ramus' mockery or even his dismissal. Whatever happened, it's not entirely impossible that the rumour was started by William Ramus in order to get back at the family who had fired him. The newspapers were quick to jump on this unexpected development, of course.

> 'Poor Billy Ramus! – The King's old confidential Page! the constant fore-runner, harbinger, and partaker of His Majesty's pleasurable excursions! – He and his companions discarded! suddenly and unexpectedly! – to make room for new faces!'[7]

In stark contrast to mocking the king's indisposition, wrote *The Morning Post and Advertiser*, 'in regard to MR. RAMUS, it is necessary to state that he never was permitted to attend on his Majesty from the day before his late infirmity was first visible, to the present moment, so it is impossible that he could have been guilty of any imprudent communications, though he has equally suffered with the others [the several other pages who were dismissed] for an offence which most probably existed only in the imaginations of their vile traducers.'[8]

Innocent or not, Ramus wasn't a wet behind the ears new arrival. He had already spent several years in George's service at the time he was given his marching orders and was well liked by the Prince of Wales as well as the king. Ramus was from a loyal and faithful family who had served the monarch well through thick and thin, and George III would turn to him for advice on the mood of the country whenever he needed 'the man in the street's' take on things. Ramus, it was claimed, could even anticipate the next target of the caricaturists and printmakers who could make or break a reputation in Georgian Britain.

With this in mind, Ramus and the other pages presented their grievances to the queen, lamenting that they had been dismissed despite having done nothing wrong. In fact, they believed that they had been removed from service at precisely the moment when they might be needed most. Perhaps it was this that caused a change in the king's heart because once the sovereign recovered his wits and his spirits he considered the fate of William Ramus and was troubled by the thought that this formerly loyal and caring servant might suffer in the future because of his embarrassingly public dismissal. George granted Ramus an annuity and gave him a glowing reference which allowed the former page to join the staff of Charles Cornwallis, the Governor-General of India.

> 'Mr. Ramus has received the most flattering recommendations from his Majesty, and some of the younger branches of the Royal Family to Lord Cornwallis; and it is supposed will, soon after his arrival in Calcutta, be invested with an honour and lucrative employment. Mr. Ramus departs with the first ship for Bengal, and if any thing could console him under the loss of an immediate attendance on his Majesty, it is the warm and liberal manner in which his Royal Master espouses the interests of his present destination.'[9]

So now we have a motive, a man named Ramus and even a trip to India.

Of course, should we wish to give credence to the secret daughter theory, we might argue that William Ramus' relocation to India was spectacularly well-timed to allow him to take young Eliza with him. After all, India was precisely where she supposedly grew up in the care of her paternal family. Yet Ramus didn't travel straight away as ill health detained him in England for some time. He didn't recover until 1790 and when he finally did start his new life in India, there is no record of there being a child at his side. Ramus died in 1792, taking his part in the story – if indeed he had any part in the story – to the grave with him.

The facts, such as they are, would tend to support whichever version of the story we choose to believe. Either there was a daughter born and William Ramus was spirited off to India to raise her, or there was no little girl and Ramus made an ill-judged comment in the heat of the moment that kickstarted the rumours and linked his name to that of Princess Elizabeth forevermore. Personally, though the story has all the ingredients of a great tale, I'm not convinced by its veracity. Elizabeth, I believe, was nothing more than a sickly young lady who fell foul of the Georgian rumour mill. She wouldn't be the first, after all!

An Intruder

> 'Spang, a hair-dresser, got clandestinely into the Queen's Palace, with a design of making love to the Princess Elizabeth; for which he was confined in Bedlam.'[10]

As 1788 drew on, and Princess Elizabeth's constitution became stronger, her father languished in the grip of his own ruinous illness. A sense of gloom descended over the castle and for loyal retainers such as Frances Burney, it became necessary to affect an air of innocence when it came to the cause of that pall. As princesses and the queen suffered with nervous maladies, it was better to try and jolly people along rather than speculating on the state of the king's health or the royal marriage. If not *quite* unexplained, Burney and the queen's ladies claimed to be in the dark as to the reason behind the shared anxiety, or rather they 'thought it necessary to seem so.'

It was a trying time for the family, and for Princess Elizabeth, there was a frightening and unexpected incident to deal with on top of everything else. A decision had already been taken not to tell Elizabeth of Margaret Nicholson's attempt on the life of the king in case the shock of the news caused her spasms to return. Unfortunately, there was also to be an attempt on Elizabeth herself.

On 29 April, as the princess was relaxing in her room at the Queen's House, the door opened and a stranger burst in. The frightened young woman sprang to her feet and dashed from the room. She called for help and a page came running to detain the intruder. He meant no harm, he said, and wished only to deliver a message to the king that God had personally entrusted him with. The unnamed man was taken to the porter's lodge where the porter admitted that he had never seen him before in his life. With that, the intruder was thrown out.

Just like Mr Stone, the Princess Royal's would-be suitor, this stranger on a mission from God wouldn't take no for an answer.

That same afternoon the unwelcome and unwanted visitor returned to the palace. This time he didn't break in but instead asked to be personally introduced to Princess Elizabeth so 'That he might pour out the ardency of his passion, and at her feet press for an equal return.'[11] This time, unsurprisingly, he was detained for further questioning.

The princess' admirer was taken into custody and finally introduced himself as Henry Spang. The heavenly messenger was in fact a hairdresser who worked for a Mr Warren in Paved Alley off Pall Mall and lodged a short walk from the Strand. As Spang was being transported to Bow Street for questioning, the guards stopped in at Paved Alley and asked Mr Warren to confirm their prisoner's story. On seeing his employer, the previously mild-mannered Spang spat in his face. Clearly there was no love lost there. Warren was perplexed. He explained that Spang had been in his employ for two uneventful years then just upped and left one week earlier, giving no notice. Spang was an honest and steady fellow, said Warren, who was bewildered as to how he had changed so much in such a short time.

At Bow Street, when Spang was asked how he came to gain access to the Queen's House he replied, 'aye, that is the question', but he refused to give an actual answer. He mocked the porter who couldn't explain how an intruder had passed without being seen and apprehended. Shortly afterwards 'the head porter at the Queen's-house, and one of the under porters, [were] dismissed, in consequence of the late intrusion into the Princess Elizabeth's apartment, by Spang, the maniac.'[12]

Spang, it transpired, had been detained before after suffering a mental breakdown, something Mr Warren had been unaware of. On being asked whether he had committed the break-in because he loved Princess Elizabeth, Spang replied that he was in love not just with her, but with all the world. When questioned about his background, he explained that his father had been a Dane and that he did indeed have living relatives. They were the Dukes of Cumberland, Gloucester, and York, as well as the King of Spain. As far as Spang was concerned, he had committed no crime, for his self-proclaimed royal blood meant that he had every right to pass freely through the royal household. It was his palace as much as it was theirs.

In fact, Spang had been a hairdresser for a number of years in London, where he had once serviced illustrious clients. A period of insanity had seen him confined to first one workhouse and then another, and he even spent time in a straitjacket. The newspapers reported that Spang was in his late-twenties and certainly no older than 30. He was gentle and not at all aggressive, but he was visibly nervous. Spang's build was short, his hair and skin fair, and his clothes were shabby as befit a man of his lowly station. When he was taken into custody by the members of the queen's guard, he was carrying no weapon and had not a single penny in his pockets. He was distraught at his situation and wept openly throughout the questioning.

What was to be done with him?

Eventually Spang was committed to the care of the Covent Garden watch, where he was to remain on the off chance that someone might come to claim him. If they did, he would be moved to his home parish, rather than remain at the expense of Londoners. However, during his incarceration orders were given - by who we can't be sure - that he should be cared for with tenderness and understanding in his own apartment. Given the king's gentle response to both Nicholson and Stone, it's not hard to imagine that these instructions might have come from George III himself.

When questioned once again over why he was in the apartments of Princess Elizabeth, Spang had no answer. In fact, in the short space of time that had passed following his arrest, he had completely forgotten who Elizabeth was and nothing that was said could jog his memory. He was dazed and confused, lost in his own reality.

Of course, nobody came to claim the unfortunate Henry Spang and he joined Nicholas and Stone in Bedlam, never to see the princess or her family again. Yet for the royal household, the end of the strange case of

Henry Spang seemed to be the final chapter in their misfortunes for a time. Elizabeth's health was improving, the various bouts of whooping cough, measles and other ailments that had plagued the royal children came to an end, and miracle of miracles, the king's wits had been restored. This meant that the closed doors of the palace were to be opened– or as open as they had ever been under George and Charlotte – and the girls could one again venture forth.

Within reason.

Farmer Elizabeth

When the three elder sisters accompanied the king and queen to the south coast on a trip designed to bolster George's health and whip up public morale, Augusta was in her element as she watched the sailors perform their nautical duties. Unlike her sister, Elizabeth far preferred to spend her time a little further in land. She, like her father, was more about the life agricultural than the life aquatic.

Elizabeth and Queen Charlotte eventually found their favourite refuge at Frogmore in Windsor. Their relationship with the house began in 1790 when Queen Charlotte sought the assistance of Lord Harcourt to secure the Crown lease on so-called Little Frogmore, a parcel of land and a cottage within the estate. Charlotte renamed the cottage Amelia Lodge in honour of her youngest daughter and set about creating the retreat she longed for. Bruised and laid low by the time she had spent caring for her husband during his illness, Charlotte relished the opportunity of filling her time with this new project, and her love of botany that had turned Kew into a gardener's paradise now transformed Frogmore too.

Two years after Charlotte obtained the lease on Little Frogmore, she added the estate of Great Frogmore to her property portfolio. Eventually Amelia Lodge would be demolished, and the queen's favourite retreat would become Frogmore Cottage. It was Queen Charlotte's home away from home, a little place where she and her elder daughters could safely occupy their very own secluded bubble. And nobody showed more enthusiasm for the Frogmore project than Princess Elizabeth.

At Frogmore, Elizabeth could let her imagination run riot. In the years to come and with the aid of architect James Wyatt, Princess Elizabeth envisioned and created dramatic follies to decorate the grounds of the house. Highly fashionable during the Georgian era, follies were an attempt to recreate a dreamy, classical landscape that would transport visitors to another time and place – well suited for the secluded, frustrated princesses. She was also the designer behind the intricately decorated Frogmore hermitage and when festivities were held at the retreat, it was Elizabeth who assumed responsibility for decorating them with 'bay leaves and artificial flowers, wreaths of flowers decorating the intermediate spaces at the top: the chandeliers suspended from the ceiling were in the shape of a bee-hive: at the upper end of them formed the tassel; between each row of lamps were interwoven ears of corn, blue bells, violets, lilies of the valley.'[13] So short-sighted as to be virtually blind without the spectacles she started to wear, it must have been a labour of love indeed for Elizabeth, and one not undertaken lightly.

In fact, just like Augusta's pining for a nautical life, one can't help but feel a pang at the talent Elizabeth had and the fact that it rarely found its expression outside of her family circle. Though she did publish books, as we'll learn later, it feels as though she might have gone much further if she'd been born male or in a different time and place. Of course, a princess can only play the cards she's dealt.

'The Princess Royal, and Princess Elizabeth, were arrived at maturity,' wrote John Britton, 'and ever incited by their Domestic Mother to indulge rather in rural amusements than the crowded and oppressive metropolitan ball-room'[14] and Elizabeth was happy to comply. She established a little farm at Frogmore and among the animals bred there were 'Pigs [that are] of the Chinese breed', a fashionable creature amongst the Georgians. Don't be fooled into thinking that the farm was merely a bit of frippery to entertain a spoiled princess either. Elizabeth might have referred to it in a letter to her friend, Lady Mary Osborne, as 'my Hobby Horse,' but in fact it was a working concern. Lands were rented out and when Lady Holderness wished to purchase a couple of quality pigs of her own, it was to Princess Elizabeth that she turned.

For the king and queen, to see their daughter devoted to such wholesome pursuits was a welcome distraction from the activities of their sons. This time it was Prince Augustus Frederick's turn to scandalise the household, much to everyone's surprise. Whilst visiting Rome, the young man met Lady Augusta Murray, the daughter of John Murray, 4th Earl of Dunmore. Under the terms of the Royal Marriages Act, any child of George III had to seek the permission of their father to wed or the marriage would be invalid, but Augustus Frederick was having none of that. After just four romantic months, Augusta and Augustus were married by William Gunn, an English clergyman in Rome.

And the news seeped out.

As soon as the couple arrived back on British shores, they repeated the marriage ceremony and not long afterwards, Augusta gave birth to the first of their two children. By now fully recovered from his malady, the king was utterly apoplectic. Though Augustus was without a doubt one of his favourite children, he had overstepped the mark badly.

George banished Augustus, who was then 20, back to Italy and had Augusta and her mother hauled before the Privy Council to be questioned on the circumstances that had led to the marriage. Though the press and public rallied behind the star-crossed lovers to call for clemency, the king wouldn't be swayed. In 1794, he had the marriage annulled. The prince was out of favour, and as proof of this, all of the princesses were forbidden from writing to him lest his bad behaviour somehow rub off on them. At a time when the thoughts of the three older daughters were turning towards marriage, it was the worst thing that could have happened.

Whilst all of this was going on, a rueful Princess Elizabeth wrote of the various dramas amongst her brothers:

> 'It is a mistake *my* living at Court; it was certainly intended that I should live in the Country, and been a younger brother's Wife, for I do not understand *Court* quarrels; kiss and make friends should be one of the mottos for a Palace.'[15]

Perhaps tellingly, the princess known to her siblings as Fatima signed her letter, *Cinderella*.

Whilst the marriage of Royal was being negotiated, Princess Elizabeth was considering not a real lover, but matters of fictional romance. In 1795 she produced a book entitled *The Birth and Triumph of Cupid*, published under the pseudonym of Lady Dashwood. The book was a collection of papercuts made by Elizabeth that were then engraved by Peltro William Tomkins, the court engraver. The publication was financed by George III and dedicated to Queen Charlotte. The following year it was reissued as *The Birth and Triumph of Love*, this time accompanied by poems by James Bland-Burges, a courtier who had been inspired to pick up his pen by the illustrations of the princess. The same Bland-Burges, you may remember, who had ruminated on the Princess Royal's deepening depression when she contemplated the possibility of a lonely spinsterhood in the months immediately before her unexpected betrothal.

The New Century

For Elizabeth, the new century began much as it had for Augusta. Little had changed. The girls were still employed as their mother's confidantes and their father would shortly be confined once again with a recurrence of his madness after being well for 15 years. Just like her elder sisters, Elizabeth knew that there was only way she could escape. Recalling the lyrics of a popular ballad she sighed '[how I] long to be married, [before] my beauty decays'. In fact, though the princess might have treated the subject with a wry sense of humour, there is perhaps more than a little truth behind her teasing. Put simply, without marriage her fate was already written, and every day would pass much as the one before it and the one before that. In a world in which her brothers were off fighting, romancing and living life, it was stifling.

With every year that passed, Princess Elizabeth grew a little older and in the world of dynastic marriages, the age of the bride was everything. She had to be able to provide her husband – if ever there was to be one – with an heir and the chances of that were dwindling with each passing birthday. Instead she had her farm and her art and her collection of ceramics and in 1806 she published another collection of etchings, *The Power and Progress of Genius*, adding to her intellectual achievements. Elizabeth was talented, sparky and filled with life but what the princess really wanted was a husband, because how else would she ever see the world beyond Windsor?

No sooner had Elizabeth told her eldest brother, the Prince of Wales, that 'we go on vegetating, as we have done for the last twenty years of our lives'[16], than that changed. Quite out of nowhere, she learned that she at last had a suitor.

In 1793 Louis Philippe, the Duke of Orléans, had fled France and travelled as far as America, where he had met and befriended Elizabeth's brother Edward, Duke of Kent. Louis Philippe came to England and took up residence in Twickenham, where he embarked on a career as a schoolteacher – quite a thing for the man who would one day reign as King of the French.

Despite plenty of entanglements with women, the French duke remained single. His life in England was a far cry from the opulence of the Bourbon court and he hoped to improve his position by making a good marriage. A Catholic and one with precious little to his name thanks to the French Revolution, Louis Philippe must have known that his chances weren't great, but still he persevered. Elizabeth wrote to the Prince of Wales to let him know that she had heard of Louis Philippe's interest and, crucially, so too had Queen Charlotte.

> 'I was asked by the Queen whether I knew [of Louis Philippe's interest and] I had flattered myself that from my constant steady attendance upon my mother, with my natural openness of character, I had hoped she would have had confidence in me at my time of life, but finding alas to my grief that was not the case I thought it more honourable by her and just towards myself to let her know I was not ignorant of what had passed, with my sentiments and feelings upon it.
>
> If there is no possibility of the thing *now*, I only entreat of you as the person, both from inclination, duty and affection we must look up to, that you will not dash the cup of happiness from my lips.
>
> Yet, believe me, whatever I may feel at present, and flattered at having been thought of, if I did not hope, I flatter myself I might make *them* [Louis Philippe] happy, I would not think of it, and being without any soul near them that might worry and plague on the score of religion, I do not fear it, for you know I hate meddling, have no turn for gossiping, and being firm to my own faith I shall not plague them upon theirs.'[17]

The letter is rambling, breathless even, and Elizabeth closes by asking her brother to burn the pages, but in the mention of her mother we can already see why the proposed marriage went no further. The king was vehemently opposed to his children being wed to Roman Catholics and his nerves, so delicately balanced, were at constant risk of collapse. The panicked princess begged the prince to seek a private meeting with her at which she would impart a good number of things she had discovered 'had been brought forward and rejected without a word from us, and therefore we all felt the sun of our days was set.' Put simply, the princesses had somehow discovered that their parents had quietly and comprehensively spiked any proposal that they might have received.

How she could be so sure about this is a mystery but Queen Charlotte, filled with temper and fury, might well have let the information slip during one of her tantrums. There was nothing that even Wales could do. He was still years from being appointed Regent and Louis Philippe, at that time facing no real prospect of restoration to his throne, had precious few prospects to speak of. Charlotte wouldn't even consider the proposal. It was dismissed out of hand.

Yet one avenue remained open to Elizabeth. Under the Royal Marriages Act, any child of the monarch over the age of 25 could still pursue a marriage even if parental consent had not been given. All Elizabeth had to do was give notice of the intended marriage to the Privy Council and wait twelve months. As long as both Houses of Parliament didn't voice their official disapproval, the union could then go ahead. Elizabeth, however, chose not to further incur the wrath of her mother by taking this step. Instead the suit was withdrawn, and Elizabeth remained single, still trapped in Queen Charlotte's miserable web.

A Bride at Last

Princess Elizabeth, it seemed, was destined never to fulfil her dreams of marriage and a family of her own. In the space of just a few years the Duke of Orléans married another, Princess Amelia died, and the king's wits succumbed fully to his illness, leaving the Prince Regent to rule in his stead. All of this upheaval left Elizabeth unwell, but all was not lost. Thanks to the Regent, there was at last a glimmer of hope on the horizon for the unmarried daughters of the king and queen. The princesses were granted an allowance of £9,000, new staff members and even grand new carriages, but their day-to-day lives remained inexorably bound to their mother and father. After so long, Queen Charlotte would not have her daughters grow *flighty*.

What would she have said if she knew that one of her daughters, plump, homely Elizabeth, no less, had once said that, 'I do not believe there is such a thing as a woman being a virgin, unless she stuff herself with lead?'[18]. This wasn't a princess who was content to be forever a little girl, this was a grown woman who didn't always relish nor live up to her sweetness and light reputation.

As she settled with the family at Windsor, one gets the feeling that Elizabeth had had enough of trying to be the good princess her mother wanted. She decorated her rooms and flung herself once more into art and agriculture, hosting gatherings in the cottage in the grounds that had become her sanctuary. When Princess Augusta added her name to the letter requesting more freedom that so enraged Queen Charlotte, it was like a primal scream from a woman who could bear confinement no longer.

For all the pleas for freedom though, Queen Charlotte was determined not to let go. Her health failing, she and Elizabeth visited Bath so that both mother and daughter could benefit from the healing waters, but they were forced to return home when news of the death of Princess Charlotte of Wales reached them. The public demanded to know why the queen was in Bath when her granddaughter needed her, and by the time she reached Windsor in the dying months of 1817, her health was worse than ever.

It was during this unhappy time that the royal household received an unexpected letter from Frederick, the Hereditary Prince of Hesse-Homburg who had made a play for Augusta's hand many years earlier. In the letter, he expressed his desire to marry Elizabeth. It was a request that appeared to have come out of nowhere and it seemed that there was precious little reason for it. Elizabeth had no great wealth and she was too old to have any children, but still Frederick seemed determined to press his suit. He wanted a wife and he had settled on Princess Elizabeth as the perfect candidate.

On 28 January 1818, Elizabeth received word that the prince was not only in England but was ready to make the official offer. She dashed off a letter to the Regent and told him:

'I instantly went to Augusta and Mary, and we agreed that
I must instantly inform the Queen of it in the morning,

which I did before my sisters. She answered upon my reading the letter, "You always wished to settle and have always said that you thought a woman might be happier and more comfortable in having a home."

I answer [sic] I have ever thought so, and add that a time may come when I shall bless God for a home. In our situation there is nothing but character to look to, and Count Munster says that the Prince's is excellent. I therefore candidly wish to accept this offer.'[19]

And accept it she did. Despite Queen Charlotte's raging tears, which Princess Mary recognised as the tantrum of 'a spoilt child', the Prince Regent stood his ground. This time, the man wouldn't get away.

The Prince of Hesse-Homburg was a war hero, but he wasn't exactly swimming in cash nor, as far as the society gossips were concerned, was he much to look at. Politician William Fremantle wrote to the Duke of Buckingham that 'an uglier hound, with a snout buried in hair, I never saw,' but Elizabeth saw only the man she wished to marry and in news reports relating that 'the Prince of HESSE, who is now on a visit to the PRINCE REGENT at Brighton, is a suitor for our truly amiable Princess ELIZABETH,'[20] we can have no doubts that the public longed for her to get her happy ever after.

With the betrothal agreed for April, Elizabeth was granted a dowry of £40,000 and though her mother continued to moan and wail, the path was set. Princess Elizabeth and the man she came to know as *Bluff* were wed on the evening of 7 April 1818 in the Queen's House. Elizabeth was resplendent in a gown of 'very rich and elegant silver tissue, with two broad flounces of the most beautiful Brussels point lace, each flounce headed with rich netted silvershells; body and sleeves superbly trimmed with Brussels point, the sleeves tastefully looped up with silver tassels; the robe of rich silver tissue, lined with white satin.'[21] Upon her head she wore a bandeau of diamonds and a plume of ostrich feathers, every inch the royal bride.

The king, of course, was not present at the wedding ceremony. Nor was the Regent, who was crippled by gout, but Queen Charlotte made an appearance despite her opposition to the marriage. Unsurprisingly for a woman to whom privacy and protocol was everything, she behaved impeccably.

The newlyweds set off for their honeymoon and left the wounded queen behind. It was to be enjoyed in the Prince Regent's lodge at Windsor, but Frederick was taken ill during the journey and had to stop on the road to be sick. The prince spent his honeymoon lounging about in his dressing gown with his pipe in his mouth and Elizabeth, never one for ceremony and showiness, was delighted with him. She wrote to the Prince Regent and thanked him for 'having given me so excellent a being, whose one thought is to make me happy.' Once the honeymoon was over the couple left for Hesse-Homburg, having first promised Queen Charlotte that they would return and visit her within the year. She wouldn't live to see the promise fulfilled.

Hesse-Homburg

In her new home, perhaps unsurprisingly, Princess Elizabeth was quick to flourish and in her renovations to the royal buildings of Homburg, she gave her artistic instinct free reign once more. At 47, although she was too old to have the children she might have longed for she could instead throw herself into the improvement and restoration of a land that had wanted for funds for far too long. Her promise to visit Queen Charlotte was not kept though, simply because Queen Charlotte didn't last another year. She died in November, just a few months after the marriage and departure of her daughter. For Elizabeth, the pain was intense. She wrote that, 'the blow is deep, and the sorrow rankles at my heart,'[22] but she now had the comfort of the husband with whom she was happy. It was a tonic.

Frederick V, Landgrave of Hesse-Homburg, died in January 1820 and his son succeeded to the title, with Elizabeth as his landgravine. She was still settling into her new role when she received word that George III had died. The principality that the new landgrave and landgravine had inherited was struggling under the weight of debt and Elizabeth's conscience wouldn't allow her to spend money on a trip to England for her father's funeral at a time when the land she was learning to love was so mired in poverty. With a heavy heart she sent word that she couldn't come home to mourn the late king.

Elizabeth missed her brother's coronation for the same reason, so imagine her delight first in 1820 when she was reunited with Royal on the continent and again in 1821 when Augusta travelled to see her. Despite the privations of Homburg, Elizabeth had come into her own. She dispensed charity and goodwill everywhere, adored her marital land and the people who lived there, and considered it very much her true home. Under her stewardship, the tiny principality began to change and grow in both fashion and fortune as Elizabeth ploughed her income into ensuring its prosperity.

Eleven years after Elizabeth married her Bluff, the landgrave fell ill with influenza and as he languished, a wound he had received years earlier on the Leipzig battlefield flared up once more. Within days he was dead, leaving his widow bereft. There was little that could comfort Elizabeth beyond the knowledge that 'no woman was ever more happy than I was for eleven years, and they will often be lived over again in the memory of the heart.'

Elizabeth decided to return to England for a visit and was on her way when King George IV, the brother who had been her rock, died. Everywhere she turned in her native land she saw reminders of him and for the first time this resilient, cheerful woman faltered under the weight of the grief she had endured. Still she pressed on as she always had and devoted herself upon her return to Homburg to her charitable endeavours, which were many. Like her niece, Queen Victoria, would do so famously, Elizabeth remained in her mourning black but unlike Victoria she didn't turn her entire life to the service of grief. She had too many charities to help for that.

Elizabeth, however, was growing old. In the wake of her husband's death she had almost lost the use of her legs from the shock and she was conscious of the creeping infirmity in both herself and her sisters, which she did her best to fight with regular, lengthy walks. She was a loving friend to the family of her husband, particularly the little nephews and nieces who she treated with indulgent adoration, and the family loved her in return. However, they were a quiet and withdrawn group and Elizabeth loved to socialise, so she visited Hanover and indulged in spa treatments to while away the days. She even made the trip back to England one last time in 1836, where she was reunited with those of her siblings who remained on those shores. It was the last visit to her homeland that Elizabeth would ever make.

'Her Royal Highness the Landgravine of Hesse Hombourg (better known in England as the Princess Elizabeth), aunt of the Queen, died here last night of an inflammation of the bowels.'[23]

Elizabeth fell ill on 14 January 1840 and died the very next day, aged 69. The people of the country she had taken to her heart and had called 'my own dear little Hombourg [sic]' turned out in their droves to watch her funeral procession pass by. She was buried in the Hesse-Homburg family vault, laid to rest in the place that had become her loved and loving home.

Act Five

Princess Mary, Duchess of Gloucester and Edinburgh
(25 April 1776 – 30 April 1857)

The First of the Last

The birth of Princess Mary, the eleventh child born to Charlotte and George, was the first in the second trio of royal daughters. Into the well-drilled routine of the nursery she came, the latest on a conveyor belt designed to style the princesses into perfect models of royal propriety and just like her sisters, she was expected to excel. Mary was widely considered to be the prettiest of all the princesses and Mrs Delany tells us that she had a fine singing voice, which Frances Burney recalled her putting to good use in duets with Elizabeth, but there was little that set her childhood apart from that of the three girls who had been born before her.

Immersed as the three younger girls were in their schooling, they didn't join their parents and the elder princesses on trips taken for the good of the king's recovery from his first bout of illness. They even missed out on the delights of that prolonged trip to Weymouth and the south that had caused Royal to wonder at all that she and her sisters had missed whilst cloistered at home. Instead they were left at Kew in the care of Lady Charlotte Finch. From there, the letters regularly came and went, full of instructions on life in the nursery and the schoolroom as Queen Charlotte kept an eye on her girls even from a distance. Little Mary, known to her family as *Minny*, charmed everyone she met with her cheerful nature and Mrs Delany remembered their first meeting when Mary, having forgotten her name, welcomed her by exclaiming, 'How do you do, *Duchess of Portland's friend*?". It was a lightness of character that never deserted her.

Unfortunately, Kew was precisely the place where Mary's idyllic, if somewhat regimented childhood, was to come to a shuddering halt. Like her sisters before her, she had benefitted from the king's gentleness and playful nature and when his illness left him unable to see her, she fretted and searched the house for him. Mary would ask to be picked up and held in the window so that she might look out for her father, gazing hopelessly into the grounds. When she was told that he was not yet able to visit, she asked her mother to send a message. Little Mary asked the queen to tell her father, 'Minny say Goody Papa, poor Papa.' It was a child's attempt to bring some gentle comfort to a parent who was battling with an illness that she couldn't hope to understand.

'Dear little Minny remains quite uneasy about not finding you anywhere in the House,' Charlotte told her husband as he convalesced. 'Every coach she sees is papa coming, and nothing satisfies her hardly but sitting at the window to look for you.' In fact, *Minny* was still a child in 1788 when her father was hit by a bout of madness so severe that it led Britain to the brink of a Regency. Mary was entering adolescence and she saw first-hand just how badly the father who had been so loving and yet so mysteriously absent was suffering. Although theirs was a household where talking things over wasn't exactly encouraged, she can't have missed the horror of the situation. In the hope that Mary's companionship might help, she was taken to visit George in his rooms and listened as he rambled and wept, her mother constantly tensed and ready to leap in and intervene should she be needed. All of this must have made a considerable impact on a young and intelligent girl such as Mary, who was well able to recognise suffering when confronted with it. Despite these experiences, she somehow maintained her sunny demeanour and was as outgoing and lively as Royal had been timid and reserved, but one encounter in particular cannot have failed to move her.

Perhaps recalling how she had once begged to be lifted into the window to look for her father, as the king sank further into his delusions it was decided that the sheer sight of his beloved daughters might restore him. Accordingly, Mary and Amelia were held up to the window as George strolled in the garden. On seeing the girls, he threw off his hat and began crying hysterically as he fled from their sight. For the daughters of such a loving father, it must have been shattering.

A Young Lady

Princess Mary made her first appearance at court in 1791 when she was 15. Ever effusive when it came to the royal youngsters, Frances Burney wrote that, 'She looked most interesting and unaffectedly lovely. She is a Sweet creature, and perhaps, in point of beauty, the first of this truly beautiful race, of which Princess Mary may be called pendant to the Prince of Wales.' It's true that she was certainly the only one of the princesses to be truly considered a beauty and it's true also that this quality, prized so highly among royal mothers when it came to making a good match, would lend Mary no advantage whatsoever thanks to her parents' increasing unwillingness to seek a husband for any of their girls.

Mary was supposed to make her debut leading the dancing with her brother, the Duke of Clarence. Clarence, however, got utterly sloshed and poor Mary's dreams of a glittering debut were dashed. She was destined to sit out the first dance as Clarence rolled and swayed, telling everyone that he was quite sober, because he would *hate* to get drunk and upset his sister. Mary had other men in her life who could leap to her rescue and as Clarence reeled and staggered, one young man who didn't let her down was her cousin. He was Prince William Frederick, heir to the Dukedom of Gloucester and Edinburgh.

William was born in 1776 to George III's brother, Prince William Henry, and his mother was the scandalous Maria Walpole. Though born of illustrious stock to a famed family, Maria's parents never actually married, and this of course meant that she was illegitimate. When William married Maria in 1766 the couple decided that they would keep their match a secret rather than incur George's wrath. Although the Royal Marriages Act – itself occasioned by the secret marriage of another of George's brothers – hadn't yet come into being, both bride and groom knew that the king would never approve of their union. It was better to just say nothing and avoid the fallout. The couple maintained the secret for six years and it was only once the Act had been passed that William revealed the truth about his relationship with Maria to George III. Unable to apply the Act retrospectively and annul the marriage, the furious king instead banished the couple from his presence, and they were forced to travel abroad to escape their debts. It was during these travels that Prince William Frederick was born, three months before Mary's birth, having been delivered in Rome.

William Frederick and Mary developed a mutual attraction that would endure for decades. Though he never approached George III with a proposal, it's likely that none would have been accepted anyway given his parentage. Don't forget his name, because William Frederick would return to assume a vital importance in Mary's life in twenty years' time. For the time being though, theirs would remain an unfulfilled longing, and one that William Frederick sought to exorcise with passionate affairs when he travelled to the continent. Stuck at home, his cousin could only grin and bear it.

Mary was just 20 when she met her second cousin, Prince Frederick of Orange-Nassau, who was in exile in London with his family. He was a couple of years younger, but Frederick and Mary took to one another immediately. For a time, he dared to hope that they might be married, but the writing was already on the wall for the prince in exile. Just like Augusta before her, Mary's hopes were shattered by the still-unmarried status of Royal. Once again, the king decreed, no daughter would be allowed to wed until the eldest had made her match.

Sadly, Frederick never found another to replace Mary in his affections and he died in 1799 of a fever. He was just 24. In deference to Mary's grief she was permitted to go into mourning for the man she had loved and lost. It was a small but significant allowance.

A Quiet Life

Princess Mary wasn't the loudest or the feistiest of her sisters, but she was considered an easy young lady to get along with and in Amelia, the youngest of the royal children, she found a close friend. Amelia's health was often fragile, as we'll see, and through her many trials, Mary was always there to care for her. In fact, Mary carved out a place for herself as Amelia's nurse. It was something to fill the days, after all.

Amelia and Mary couldn't have been more different. It could only lead to trouble as fiery Amelia often lost her temper with the saintly Mary. Alongside Lady Charlotte Finch and the beloved Gouly, the team of ladies who attended to the princesses included a Miss Jane Gomm, who had been a respected courtier for almost two decades and before that, had spent years living in Prussia. Well-drilled in protocol and propriety, Miss Gomm was a steady and watchful presence around the young princesses and when she became suspicious that Princess Amelia had grown rather fond of an equerry called Charles FitzRoy, she was scandalised. It wasn't something Miss Gomm could keep to herself and she shared her worries about the princess and the equerry with Princess Mary, Amelia's close friend. A worried Mary whispered her own concerns about the situation to Gouly and somehow the gossip found its way back to the queen, who confronted her youngest daughter. Never one to hold her tongue, Amelia was furious that Mary had shared her private business with one of their ladies. For the first time, the relationship between the two sisters grew strained and it looked like an all-out sibling war might be on the cards.

On this occasion, perhaps surprisingly, it was Charlotte who took it upon herself to calm the troubled waters. She reminded the livid Amelia that Mary had spoken to Gouly only because of her concern, not in the spirit of malicious gossip. Indeed, should Amelia require more evidence of Mary's kindness and love for her, she should remember that 'when You were Confined with those Boils, and could not go to Windsor, She offered of Her own Account to stay with you, as she was sure You would feel uneasy to be left alone.'

And with the mention of the boils, it seems the sisterly friendship was restored. Of Gouly and Gomm, however, Amelia remained suspicious. She would never trust them again.

Intriguingly, despite Mary's celebrated good looks and her brief and swiftly curtailed dalliance with the short-lived Prince of Orange, she didn't have the same trickle of would-be suitors beating a path to the royal door as her sisters had known. Perhaps by this point, with Royal alone married and that only after a great deal of tussle, the fact that the king and queen weren't keen on entertaining would-be bridegrooms had started to sink at in the courts of Europe. There was *one* potential candidate for Mary's hand though, and he was from the very bosom of the queen's family.

In 1805 Charlotte's brother, Charles II, Grand Duke of Mecklenburg-Strelitz, believed that the time was right for his eldest son and heir, George, to marry. By now in his mid-twenties and with excellent prospects, George was well-travelled and well-liked, and he would, Charles believed, make an excellent husband for any of the unwed princesses. He wrote to his sister, Charlotte, and she forwarded the letter to her husband with the following note:

> 'Your Majesty will see that my Brother wishes to see His Son settled, and anxiously desires him to Marry one of the younger Princesses, but as He is inclined to let him follow His own inclination, He proposes with Your leave to send him over to England, that He may make his own choice, provided Your Majesty gives him leave to do so, & that He has some hopes of Your approbation & of succeeding in his Suit. My answer, of which I also send a Copy will sufficiently prove to Your Majesty that tho as a Sister I have fairly avowed how happy such an intermarriage would make me, I have given no encouragement, but desired no step might be taken until he did hear from me.
>
> [...]
>
> I have never named the Subject to any of the Princesses, for I have made it [a] rule to avoid a Subject in which I know their oppinions [sic] differ with Your Majesty's, for every one of them have at different Times assured me that, happy as they are, they should like to settle if they could, and I feel I cannot blame them.'[1]

If you did a double take, you could be forgiven. Queen Charlotte *not* hating the idea of one of her daughters marrying and leaving home? It was virtually unheard of. Yet if we consider the queen's nature, it might not be so strange as it seems. A marriage to her own family in Mecklenburg would not only vastly increase the future prospects of the Duchy but would also keep the daughter chosen to be the bride in Charlotte's control, one way or another. Yes, she would be a wife with a husband and establishment of her own, but it would be a husband, establishment and family who were well known to Queen Charlotte, with no nasty surprises lurking around the corner. Though the lack of British support for Württemberg after the Princess Royal's marriage eventually drove *her* husband into the service of Napoleon as little more than a puppet king, I think we can safely assume that any requirements Mecklenburg might have for assistance would have been swiftly and comprehensively met, whatever it took. George, laid low by illness and always open to ideas his wife put before him, agreed to consider the matter on the condition that the girls looked on the idea of marriage favourably. The last thing he wanted was a repeat of the Caroline Matilda catastrophe.

But which princess would it be? After all, there were three younger daughters from which to choose. Of course, Amelia's ongoing health struggles and youth precluded her from being a candidate, so that left Mary and Sophia. Pulled this way and that by political conflict, the king couldn't afford to lavish too much attention on marriage plans that he didn't exactly relish to start with. The death of William Pitt the Younger in January 1806 plunged the country into political turmoil and with his health already fragile, George simply didn't have the capacity to split himself between negotiating a marriage to Mecklenburg and navigating the choppy Westminster waters. With the latter taking precedence, the former was left to founder.

Instead Mary's life continued into the nineteenth century just as it had at the close of the eighteenth century. She remained at her mother's side, caring for Amelia, keeping her sisters and her father company, visiting the theatre, applauding Mrs Siddons, the famous Georgian actress who was a family favourite, and strolling around Weymouth until she was bored rigid. On and on went the unending repetition, day after day, year after year, trying even Mary's good temper. Just as Royal had been considered a spy for the queen because of her retiring nature, Mary's own amiability cast her in a similar role amongst the younger princesses, who suspected she was 'mama's tool'. In fact, she was simply an easy-going middle child, one of so many that it was hard to stand out in a stifling and restricted world.

The Nursemaid

Just as Augusta and Elizabeth seemed destined to become the nursemaids and companions of their mother, it looked as if Mary was heading for the same fate as the attendant of her sister, Amelia. The two resided at Augusta Lodge in the grounds of Windsor and there Amelia languished as her sister, the acknowledged beauty of the family, grew older and more insular. Though we shall learn more of Princess Amelia's clandestine romance with Charles FitzRoy later in this volume, Mary's story can't be told without some reference to her own part in that intrigue, especially at the end of Amelia's life.

For the sake of propriety, FitzRoy was, of course, forbidden from spending time alone with the woman who loved him and who we might imagine he loved in return, but Mary, amiable, isolated and perhaps a little romantic, couldn't rest at the thought of it. It was she who wrote to FitzRoy to tell him that Amelia's dying words were a declaration of love for him, doing one last favour for her beloved sister. Mary was with Amelia as she died, and when Sir Henry Halford, the princess' physician, declared that Amelia was dead and asked Mary to leave the room, the stoic woman refused to go. She remained beside Amelia until Halford had finished his business then kissed her sister goodbye and went to her rooms. By this point, the king was insensible, his last visit to his ailing daughter proving the tipping point that left him incurably insane. That's an episode we'll explore later in these pages.

Yet without Amelia to care for, what would Mary do now? She mourned her sister pitifully, crying endlessly, but life had to go on even in the darkest hours of grief. When the queen ordered her children to assemble in mourning black, Mary was the only one not to do so. She couldn't bear the thought of any kind of public display so soon after the loss, even if it was only in front of the royal household. Instead she remained at Augusta Lodge, grieving. In her will, Amelia recognised Mary's loyalty and left her a quantity of jewellery, sentimental pieces for the woman who had nursed her.

Mary needed a distraction and she found it in her cheerful, strong-willed niece, Princess Charlotte of Wales. She and Princess Sophia were Charlotte's favourite aunts and in her niece's company, Mary was able to rediscover some desperately needed *joie de vivre*. The daily routine of caring for Amelia had been replaced by the new daily routine of life in Queen Charlotte's small inner circle of daughters, punctuated by occasional visits to the king, whose condition was now worse than ever before. He raved and ranted, twitched and paced, now distracted with grief at Amelia's death, then imagining that the late Alfred and Octavius still lived. Virtually blind and entirely governed by his doctors, moments of lucidity were becoming increasingly rare. It was Mary's task to write daily reports for her eldest brother on the progress – or not – of the king, so she more than anyone was aware of just how bad his health had become.

Minny absorbed it all in her usual placid way, but how sore her heart must have been. And how lonely she must have been too; not for the romantic fulfilment of a husband, she'd all but given up on that, but for the distractions of society and a life away from the court. Instead her hours were dominated by her bad-tempered mother and her capricious niece, Charlotte, who at least bought some youthful fire into the lives of the aging sisters of the *nunnery,* as Sophia had so memorably christened their home in 1812.

Carriages and liveries might have followed when the Prince of Wales became the Regent in 1811, but as we've already seen, a heartfelt letter from the sisters to their mother begging for more freedom raised the queen's ire to such a degree that only the Regent's intervention could mend the breach. Thanks to his delicate way with the queen, it was eventually agreed that the princesses could serve as chaperones to young Princess Charlotte of Wales about town and Mary, starved of society for too long, was determined to throw herself at this opportunity. The Prince Regent's careful negotiations resulted in his unmarried sisters receiving generous allowances, money that Mary used to fill her wardrobe with new clothes that she could wear in society.

But there were limits to the queen's patience and when the Prince Regent invited his sisters to accompany Princess Charlotte to the State Opening of Parliament, she hit the roof. Mary was determined to accept her brother's invitation despite her mother's protests. The very fact that this quiet and unassuming princess was seen in the House of Lords that November with her sister, Elizabeth, and niece, Charlotte, sent a clear message about how things had changed. With their father incapacitated, the princesses were finally daring to push forward and to make their own way, but Queen Charlotte wouldn't let them go unpunished. After word of an almighty scene at Windsor reached the Prince Regent, he once again attempted to hold back the tide in a letter to his mother.

> 'I have been most deeply afflicted at hearing from my sisters the strong objections which you made to their coming to town for the purpose of going to the House of Lords. I do implore you, my dearest mother, for your own happiness, for that of my sisters, and for the peace of the whole family, not to suffer the repetition of scenes so distressing and so painful to all of us.'[2]

The queen would not be so easily managed though. Just one day after her son wrote to her, she took up her pen and replied in the strongest possible terms. Charlotte summoned her martyr's skills and struck back, donning the mantle of the *real* injured party. This wasn't about control, said she, it was about showing loyalty to a king who had given his life to country and family and was not going to be sidelined in favour of his eldest son. It was an outrageous accusation and considering the sense of love and duty felt by her daughters for their father, a baseless one too.

> 'Can there be, I appeal to your own feelings, a more painful, a more horrible situation, than the one your father labours under? And it was not my duty to state to your sisters, that they having no personal duty which calls upon their presence at the House of Lords, it would show more attention to female delicacy to decline it, but left it to their option to do as they please.'[3]

So, offered the opportunity to do as they pleased, Mary and Elizabeth had bravely opted to attend the State Opening and witness their brother's big moment. When they returned home to Windsor, they found a whirlwind waiting. When Charlotte railed against their selfishness and lack of respect, Mary and Elizabeth had finally had enough. Elizabeth slammed her hand violently down upon a bible to make her point felt whilst Mary, pushed to her limit, declared that she simply couldn't keep living such a stifling life. Things only got worse a few years later when Mary took the Regent's side over plans – eventually aborted once Prince Leopold came onto the scene – to marry Princess Charlotte off to the Prince of Orange. How dare she presume to have a mind of her own?

When a ball was held at Carlton House in 1814, Mary thought nothing of upstaging her niece, Charlotte, to lead the dancing and take her turn upon the floor with some of the most illustrious guests. Princess Mary was no longer content to be the pretty yet placid one. She had reached the end of her rope.

Something had to change.

An Unexpected Proposal

> 'We are told that the Royal Nuptials between the Duke of GLOUCESTER and the Princess MARY will take place on

the 8th inst. at Carlton House. This was long a favourite object with our good old King. His MAJESTY often expressed a wish to the QUEEN on the subject. It was at last broached to the Princess MARY, and every thing is now arranging for the nuptials.'[4]

The late and scandalous Duke of Gloucester and Edinburgh died in 1805 and his son, Prince William Frederick, succeeded to the dukedom. He is perhaps best known for being the man who was first nicknamed *Silly Billy* and was also the man who young Princess Charlotte would name as a possible suitor whenever she wanted to annoy her father. The priggish, protocol-obsessed Gloucester, however, thought he might have a chance with his glamorous and highly eligible cousin. Indeed, he even went so far as to tell her that whenever she was ready, he would be waiting devotedly for her. When Charlotte's whirlwind and passionate romance with Leopold foiled his ambitions, Gloucester readjusted his sights and settled them on Princess Mary once more.

Shortly before the unexpected wedding of Mary and Gloucester, Princess Charlotte married Prince Leopold of Saxe-Coburg-Saalfeld. We can thank Leopold's friend, Baron Stockmar, for the following unflattering sketch of the duke.

> 'Duke of Gloucester - Prominent, meaningless eyes; without being actually ugly, a very unpleasant face, with an animal expression; large and stout, but with weak helpless legs. He wears a neckcloth thicker than his head.'[5]

Ten years after William Frederick became the Duke of Gloucester and Edinburgh he travelled to Brighton and sought an audience with the Prince Regent to ask for Princess Mary's hand in marriage. Mary admitted to Lady Harcourt that, 'The real truth is that, though the queen and prince gave their consent on Saturday and felt satisfied all was settled, I was not quite so myself until last night. However, I started a subject to the Duke of Gloucester that required a very decided answer before I could finally make up my mind.'[6]

I don't think we should be too surprised that Mary had her doubts and once the decision was made and her answer given she confided to Lady Harcourt that, 'I don't know what other people feel when going to be married, but as yet I have done nothing but cry.'[7] Hardly the most common reaction for a bride-to-be, I think you'll agree. For once, the queen didn't make life difficult and she seemed to have resigned herself to the match, perhaps because marriage to Gloucester meant that Mary would stay reasonably close by. There would be no distant European castle waiting for its new chatelaine in her case.

What brought Mary particular sadness was the fact that her beloved father not only didn't understand the situation but was quite unable to give his blessing to the match. When she wrote to her old friend, Lady Harcourt, she confessed that the thought of leaving Windsor and all that it contained was like a knife to her heart.

'That dear Castle,' Mary explained, 'contains all that I value in this world; that dear place [...] and the idea of leaving that *House* at Moments half breaks my heart.' To Mary, Windsor Castle had more than sentimental value. Since Willis had confined the king there, it would forever be 'the spot in which my most *valuable* & respectable Father is *incircle*d.' She freely admitted to Lady Harcourt that 'I am not to receive his Blessing and approbation, with those of all the rest of my family, [and it] half kills me.'

The Duke of Gloucester was sympathetic to his fiancée's concerns and promised that she would never be kept from returning to Windsor and the bosom of her family. And so, the deal was done, and the marriage could proceed. Princess Mary was to be a bride at last.

Duchess

Mary and Gloucester married on 22 July 1816. Though the king couldn't be present in person, Mary certainly carried him in her heart, and she wore a ring containing a lock of her father's hair, believing that some terrible omen would befall her if she didn't. At 40 years old, Mary had waited so long that just like Elizabeth, she was determined to dress for the occasion. Her gown was made by the erstwhile Miss Wing of St James's, a long-time favourite dressmaker of the royal women and grandeur was the word of the day. The dress was English made, the press proudly pointed out, as was expected of every gown worn at the royal wedding.

'The wedding dress, a very rich and elegant silver tissue, with two superb borders of scolloped [sic] lama flouncing,

elegantly worked in pineapple pattern, each border headed
with three weltings of rich lama work; the body and sleeves
to correspond and tastefully trimmed with most beautiful
brussels point lace; the robe of rich silver tissue, lined with
white satin and trimmed round with superb scalloped lama
pineapple border, to correspond with dress, and fastened at
the waist with a very brilliant diamond clasp.'[8]

The day passed in a whirl of celebration and many, many tears were
shed – hopefully all of them from happiness. The Prince Regent gave
his sister away in front of guests including a Mr Provis, the Verger of
Whitehall Chapel. Many years earlier, when he served in the Chapel
Royal, the same Mr Provis had been present at Mary's christening too.
She had almost come full circle.

On the day that he became the husband of Princess Mary, the Duke
of Gloucester was finally given the title *His Royal Highness*. Now at
last he could match his new wife's rank. Though he gladly accepted this
honour, the couple declined Parliament's offer of a dowry, satisfied that
what they already had would be enough.

'The Princess MARY and attendants left [Windsor] Castle
on Thursday evening for London. Her Royal Highness
appeared much affected, as it was understood she was taking
her farewell of the Castle as her residence previous to her
marriage. Her Royal Highness took an affectionate leave
of Princess Sophia and the principal attendants. Numbers
of the servants and inhabitants of Windsor attended to
take their respectful leave, and made their obeisance, her
Royal Highness being universally beloved and respected by
all ranks.'[9]

The Duke and Duchess made their home at Bagshot Park, less than a
dozen miles from Windsor. There Mary could finally be the mistress
of her own establishment. Even better, the duke *almost* kept true to his
promise that she could see her family whenever she so wished, so she
was never too far from her parents and siblings. This wasn't the case
when it came to the Prince Regent, who Gloucester disliked intensely,
considering him to be immoral. He did all he could to create obstacles

whenever the Gloucesters were invited to spend time with the Regent and Mary wryly told her brother that, 'Man is Man, and does not like to be put out of his way, and still less by a Wife than anybody else.'

Still, Mary assured her family that she was loved and cared for by a man whose only desire in life was to see her happy. Intriguingly, she never seemed quite so effusive in her praise for Gloucester as he appears to have been for her. Gloucester disliked entertaining and with Bagshot Park in disarray, he hated to see any mess in his prized London pad of Gloucester House, so he locked up the best drawing room and spirited away the keys, forcing Mary to welcome guests in her rooms. 'The Duke of G[loucester] torments the Duchess,' wrote Sir William Gell, 'and makes her live up at the tip-top of the house.'

'I have always remarked that these half-and-half people of blood, noble or royal, are peculiarly grand,' he went on in his letter to Charlotte Campbell Bury, 'and give themselves twice as many airs as the original roots and direct branches of the tree.'[10]

How much truth there is in this we can't be sure. Princess Charlotte of Wales commented that the duke seemed happier with his bride than she was with him but she also noted that Mary was delighted to simply be the mistress of her own fate and home and revelled in being able to wander the grounds and preside over Bagshot Park. Still, perhaps marriage to the duke wasn't all she had hoped it might be when it came to love. Gloucester was a grump and a snob, obsessed with signalling his own religious virtue and piety and engaged in constant moral one-upmanship with his peers. For this reason, he and the Regent would never see eye to eye, and Gloucester doubtless knew that if Mary was ever forced to choose whose side she was on, she would stand by her brother. Hopelessly estranged from his wife, Caroline of Brunswick, the Prince Regent co-opted his sisters to serve as his social hostesses whenever possible and Mary loved it. She shone at the glittering court of the Royal Pavilion, something that must have left her husband steaming mad as he went out shooting to fill the days that Mary spent partying with her brother. I wonder whose face he was picturing on his quarry.

Perhaps in an effort not to have to spend too long in one another's company, the duke and duchess embarked on a tour of the estates and townhouses of their friends. Once trapped in the nunnery at Windsor, Mary rejoiced at becoming a belated part of the giddy Regency social scene. She would be hidden away no longer.

If her husband wasn't all that Mary might have wished him to be, one might say the same about Bagshot Park. The house was desperately in need of renovation, but repairs meant money. Having refused a dowry when they married, now the couple asked the Regent if they could have some assistance to improve their living conditions. Of course he said yes and as Bagshot Park was finally given the TLC it needed so badly, green-fingered Mary set to work in the grounds. She was creating a sanctuary at last.

Siblings and Spouses

As Mary settled into her marriage and the management of Bagshot and its ongoing renovations, she found that her husband wasn't always present. Gloucester's military and diplomatic duties often called him abroad and he told his wife that he had no expectation that she would travel with him and nor, if things were as difficult as some claimed, did she want to. By now, Queen Charlotte's health was in terminal decline and the Gloucesters believed that the best course of action was for Mary to stay close to her mother in what looked likely to be her final months.

Elizabeth and Royal were now mistresses of their own foreign courts, Amelia was dead and only Augusta and Sophia remained to complete the little cabal that had once been gathered so tightly around the queen. Mary became a nurse to Charlotte just as she had once cared for Amelia. She was with her mother when she died and though the death left her grieving, it was nothing compared to her misery when George III died the following year. Even after she departed for Bagshot Park Mary had made frequent visits to Windsor and doted on her father as much as ever. Despite his illness, the thought of his death was abhorrent to her. As she explained to Lady Harcourt, 'life indeed would be a burthen [sic] to us poor Girls without him.'

Yet that dreaded day was swiftly approaching and just a week after the death of Mary's brother, the Duke of Kent, King George III died. The death of Kent, a man who had seemed to be in the prime of life, was unexpected. In contrast, that of the king had been on the cards for a long time. Despite this, Mary was shaken by his passing, utterly unprepared 'for the loss of any one one *loves*, & the *Blow* was as great I am sure to all of us as if it had been an unexpected *Calamity*. The loss of such a father & such a King will long be felt.' For what remained of her long life, Mary would always celebrate on 4 June with a party held in honour of the birthday of her late father. She took the furniture that had once been in her rooms at Windsor and moved it into Bagshot, recreating that familiar landscape in her marital home.

But now there was to be a new king. And Mary's husband hated him.

What this meant, of course, was that the Regent was the Regent no longer, but King George IV. When George III died, the heir to the throne was laid low himself with a serious cold that threatened his own life. Luckily for him, he survived and rallied just in the nick of time, though he was far too sick to attend the funeral of his late father. He wasn't too sick to become king though.

How Gloucester must have rankled to see the man he hated in such an exalted position. It's almost tempting to say he might have been cheesed off.

And things were getting worse.

When Caroline of Brunswick returned to Britain to face the Pains and Penalties Bill, which was George IV's attempt to divorce her and strip her of rank and title, Mary was firmly on her brother's side. The Duke of Gloucester, meanwhile, believed that Caroline was the injured party and forbade Mary to visit or write to George as long as the trial went on. It was a slight that stung both the princess and the king, and George was conspicuously ungenerous with honours for the Duke of Gloucester. Indeed, it wasn't until 1827 that he finally saw fit to hold out an olive branch, appointing Gloucester Governor of Portsmouth. Perhaps he was going soft in his old age.

As the older members of the family passed away one by one and Mary's siblings were lost to her, she took comfort instead in the company of the young Princess Victoria, who she was very close to. Mary saw three kings die – her husband and two of her brothers – and was in her dotage by the time her beloved niece took to the throne as Queen Victoria. Victoria would eventually honour the memory of her beloved aunt in the name of her own daughter, Beatrice Mary Victoria Feodore.

In 1834, eighteen years after their marriage, the Duke of Gloucester fell ill. The first signs of his malady appeared just a few weeks before as he and Mary were hosting hundreds of children from charity schools and treating them to a feast of roast beef and beer. Though the duke hadn't reported feeling unwell, some of those present commented on how sickly he looked. They were to be proved right.

As autumn deepened into winter, the Duke of Gloucester took to his bed at Bagshot Park and declined at a rapid rate. He was just 58 and the newspapers reported that he was suffering with a bilious fever. There was little hope entertained of his recovery by Sir Henry Halford, who was leading the physicians at the duke's bedside.

As she watched her husband decline within the walls of Bagshot Park, Mary was accompanied by her sister, Sophia. Constant updates were sent to Victoria and Albert, who were holidaying in Brighton. Day after day came the bulletins and every time the report was the same: no worse, no better, no hope.

> 'The Duke of GLOUCESTER expired at his residence in Bagshot Park, at twenty minutes before seven o'clock on Sunday evening. [...] The Duchess of GLOUCESTER and the Princess SOPHIA MATILDA remained yesterday at Bagshot. The Duchess was stated to be as well as could be expected considering the anxiety and fatigue her Royal Highness has undergone during the last fortnight.'[11]

Just like that, the duchess could descend from her confinement on the upper floors of Gloucester House and show off her homes at last. She remained at Bagshot after Gloucester's passing and there enjoyed the company of her sister, Sophia, as well as Victoria and eventually Albert and their children too. When Princess Elizabeth visited from the continent to comfort the new widow, she was surprised to find that Mary was in high spirits, not only as well as could be expected but perhaps better even than that.

In the rooms that had once been locked and forbidden to her, Mary hosted social gatherings and philanthropic events for family and friends alike. Yet it wasn't all fun and games and when Victoria ascended the throne, Mary found herself caught in the crossfire between the new queen and Mary's brother, Ernest, the new King of Hanover. And he knew how to make trouble.

When Queen Charlotte died, a quantity of her jewels had been entrusted to the keeping of the monarch and so long as Great Britain and Hanover shared a ruler all was well. With the death of William IV in 1837, that situation changed. Salic law meant that Victoria could inherit the throne of Great Britain but no woman could rule in Hanover, so the crowns were divided, and Ernest took the latter. He believed that this meant he was also entitled to the jewels that had once belonged to his mother and he was determined to claim them as his own. The legal saga of the jewellery was one that ran for years and Mary was asked who she thought should be the rightful keeper of the jewels. She plumped loyally for her brother, who she honestly thought had more of a claim to them as the son of their original owner, Charlotte.

'I hear the little Queen is loaded with my diamonds,' roared the furious Ernest as he declared war on Victoria, and she wasn't pleased to learn that her aunt had sided with the King of Hanover. Eventually the court sided with him too and Victoria was forced to commission replicas of the pieces she liked and return the originals to him. Those replicas eventually went on to form part of the Crown Jewels collection.

Happily, Mary and Victoria's relationship survived as the Duchess of Gloucester grew older. Eventually she left Bagshot and moved to White Lodge, which allowed her to be closer to the ailing Sophia. The sisters were coming together once more.

The Last Daughter

With Sophia's death in 1848, Mary alone remained of the daughters of George III and Charlotte of Mecklenburg-Strelitz. She and Sophia had been able to support each other through the death of Princess Augusta eight years earlier but now no sister remained to hold Mary's hand as she grieved for Sophia. It seemed as though Sophia's death was something of a full stop for Mary too and her own health – but not her spirits - went into a slow decline. She began to suffer periods of confusion, evident from a note in Queen Victoria's journal that her aunt was 'seized with giddiness & faintness' during the christening of the queen's daughter, Princess Louise. It was an early indication of what was to follow.

Unsurprisingly, given that they had stuck together through thick and thin, Mary's grief at the death of her sister and best friend, Sophia, was immense. Yet Victoria was always on hand to serve as friend and companion and the queen's journals make frequent reference to walks and lunches with her Aunt Mary. Even as she buried more and more of her kin, the inquisitive Mary embraced the modern age and was fascinated by the Great Exhibition, which she visited on several occasions. She remained as sprightly as her health would allow but as the world moved faster, Mary was markedly slowing down.

> 'To survive prejudice and live down calumny, to be denounced as a tyrant abroad, and to be respected as the most truly constitutional Sovereign by his people – are contrarieties that seldom fall to the lot of either man or monarch. Yet such has been the fate of Ernest King of Hanover, whose earthly career was brought to a close in his palace at Herrenhausen at an early hour yesterday morning.'[12]

The death in 1851 of Ernest, King of Hanover, left Mary as the sole surviving child of that once mighty brood of fifteen. She had become a virtual grandmother, doting on the family of Victoria and Albert and fretting for them as though they were her own children as they grew into adults and set off on their own lives. Although Victoria's own mother was still alive, the relationship between mother and daughter had always been difficult.

Mary fell ill in the spring of 1857 but still she soldiered on. From her sickbed in Gloucester House, she continued to greet family and friends until the middle of April, when she fell into a state of exhaustion. She slipped in and out of conscious, clinging onto the barest threads of life as her beloved family gathered around her bedside to say goodbye.

> 'Her Royal Highness the Duchess of Gloucester expired, without suffering, at a quarter after five o'clock this morning.'[13]

Princess Mary died on 30 April 1857 at the age of 81. With her, the last threads of the court of George III were severed and in the new modern age her coffin was carried from London to Windsor not by horse and carriage, but by the Great Western Railway. For a lady who revelled in her visits to the Great Exhibition and the eye-opening discoveries it contained, it's not difficult to believe that she would have appreciated taking her final journey in so modern a fashion. It was Princess Mary to a T.

Act Six

Princess Sophia of the United Kingdom (3 November 1777 – 27 May 1848)

Growing Up

It won't come as a surprise to learn that Princess Sophia, the fifth of the six daughters of George and Charlotte, had the same unremarkable upbringing as her sisters. Of course, there was no great change in the routine by this point, no spanner in the works, nothing but the familiar faces and schedules that governed Sophia in her youth just as they had the sisters who had gone before her. Many illustrious ladies could be referenced in the chosen names of Princess Sophia but perhaps the most illustrious of all was the Electress of Hanover, mother of George I and the woman who, had she lived just a few more weeks, would have succeeded Anne as queen. Instead she died first and her son, George I, came to the throne in her place.

Sophy, as she was known to her family, doted on little Prince Octavius, who she referred to as 'my son' and his early death was the first taste of bitter reality in a life that would be full of emotional upheavals. Sophia was, I think we can assume from the following anecdote, a rather sensitive and eager-to-please child.

Among the many tutors employed to make young ladies out of the little girls was a music master named Mr Webb. This particular tutor's distinguishing feature was his nose, which was abnormally large and covered a great portion of his face, disfiguring him. Queen Charlotte was conscious that her younger children might laugh at Mr Webb and she warned them all that they mustn't react to the unusual nose in any way whatsoever. Instead, it was business as usual.

Little Sophia listened intently to her mother's instruction, taking it all on board and following it to the letter. One day, when Lady Cremorne was visiting the family, Mr Webb was announced. Sophia leapt to her feet and ran to Lady Cremorne to warn her in a whisper, 'Mr Webb has got a very great nose, but that is only to be pitied – so mind you don't laugh.' On another occasion, upon learning what prisons were, Sophia forfeited her allowance and asked if it could be donated to prisoners instead, along with an accompanying donation from her father.

Sensitive indeed for a child of just nine!

Of Sophia's early life there is little to say that hasn't already been said with regard to her sisters. Just as we have seen talents for drawing, music, singing and botany, for Sophia it was needlepoint, a perfectly ladylike pursuit for a young princess. Like her siblings, she was loyal and loving to her brothers, particularly in regard to the Prince of Wales, and she too faced her fair share of ill health. Colonel Goldsworthy, the king's equerry, blamed it on the freezing passages of Windsor and exclaimed, 'I believe in my heart there's wind enough in these passages to carry a man of war! […] Princess Elizabeth is done for [she wasn't!]; then Princess Royal begins coughing; then Princess Augusta gets the snuffles; and all the poor attendants, my poor sister at their head, drop off, one after another, like so many snuffs of candles: till at last, dwindle, dwindle, dwindle – not a soul goes to the chapel but the king, the parson, and myself; and there we three freeze together!'[1]

Not only did Sophia have the cold to contend with, but as one of the youngest daughters of the king and queen, she grew up in a world in which her father's illness was ever present. She saw first-hand his struggles and as one of his favourites, was often prevailed upon to spend time with him during his attacks. She saw too the long line of unmarried sisters who had come before her and she must have known that it was her fate to join them. Perhaps it was that sure knowledge that led her to plunge into one of the most scandalous and intriguing of all the episodes involving one of the children of George III. In the life of the quiet and unassuming Sophia we find not only a love affair, but rumours of an illegitimate child and all sorts of mystery.

And then there was the Duke of Cumberland. Of which, more anon.

Illness

'I have had the honour [the King said] of about an hour's conversation with that young lady [Sophia], in the old style; though I have given up my mad frolics now. To be sure,

I had a few in that style formerly! – upon my word I am almost ashamed! – Ha! Ha! Ha!'[2]

The king always had a particular affection for his younger children and Sophia and Amelia, the two youngest daughters, were among his favourites. As press and public speculation as to the nature of his illness grew more feverish, Sophia witnessed its symptoms first-hand when she and Queen Charlotte visited her father in his confinement. Ever ready to snatch up her children and spirit them away should the king segue into one of his sometimes inappropriate, rambling, foaming soliloquies, Charlotte would troop the girls into George's rooms and there they would attempt to give the impression that all was normal.

But all was far from normal. The gay Hanoverian court promised as a source of husbands was not to be and Sophia was soon old enough to recognise that. She was old enough too to recognise the fact that her father had changed beyond recognition. Family dinners became tense affairs. The queen grew ever more withdrawn and emotional as the weight fell off her already slender frame. Sleepless nights and worry aged her and frayed her temper even more, and the already limited horizons of the princesses became ever more restrictive.

On Sophia's eleventh birthday, the king - by now in the throes of the episode that almost led to an early Regency - was allowed to join his family for dinner. His head shaved and his skin blistered, he could barely walk even with the cane that he had taken to using and when he came to dinner, his appearance was shocking. His eyes were black and bulbous, his face swollen and his voice hoarse. Distracted and disinterested, he slept through dinner.

Yet sleeping through dinner would pale in comparison to a repeat performance just two days later. This time the king was far from sleepy but was instead possessed of the manic energy that characterised his illness. In front of the entire royal family he chattered about nothing until he foamed at the mouth. Eventually the Prince of Wales attempted to calm him, and the king dragged his son from his seat and threw him bodily across the room. As Queen Charlotte fled in hysterics with her husband in pursuit, Wales broke down in tears and his sisters were left to comfort him.

That night, the queen refused to go to her husband's room and instead summoned her daughters to her. She sat with them through the night, weeping and despairing. It was to set the pattern for many years to come.

Although the three younger girls remained at home when the elder trio and their parents set off for the restoring waters of Weymouth in 1789, perhaps it served as something of a break for them too. There would be no more experimental visits to the raving or weeping king and no more long, arduous evenings sitting in silence with the queen as they worked at needlepoint or whatever other improvement was expected of them. Instead the air was lighter and though the routine wasn't changed, the doctors and their patient were, for now at least, departed.

Sophia made her debut to celebrate the birthday of the Prince of Wales in 1792 but it was far from the start of a new glittering social life. Her health was anything but robust and she went through disturbing incidences of what were referred to in reports as *spasms*, which were quite possibly caused by anxiety. The same spasms would be attributed to Sophia throughout the next few years even as gossips sought to explain them away as something far more scandalous. She was often bedbound and even when she was allowed to join the family on later trips to Weymouth, reports came in that whilst the royal party enjoyed excursions to the harbour or down to the water, Sophia was left to languish in her bed.

It was a frustrating and dull existence for the young woman, and she was always looking for new ways to keep herself occupied. One diversion was making new friends in the royal household and she did just that when Frances Garth joined the staff as assistant governess to Princess Charlotte of Wales, the baby daughter of the Prince of Wales and his estranged wife, Caroline of Brunswick. Miss Garth was the niece of General Thomas Garth, one of the king's most trusted equerries, and she bought with her an impeccable pedigree and not the slightest hint of scandal. She and Princess Sophia soon became friends. The *other* Garth would become much, much more.

Thomas Garth

Thomas Garth was born in 1744 and joined the army at the age of 18. He rose swiftly through the ranks and by the time he was appointed as equerry to George III in 1795, he was a highly respected man both on the battlefield and off. He would remain in favour with the royal family until his death in 1829, which might seem surprising given what you're about to read.

126

As one of the king's closest aides, Garth knew the princes and princesses well. In the closing years of the eighteenth century, he often popped up in the news accompanying them here and there but reports such as 'the KING and Princess SOPHIA, accompanied by [General GARTH] rode out on horseback,'[3] are hardly the sort of things that scandals are made of. That all takes place behind closed doors.

Garth was thirty-three years older than Princess Sophia, and he was in no way a typical romantic hero. He was slight in stature and easily distinguished by the purple birthmark that covered his forehead and extended down to one eye. It was this that led Princess Mary, in a mischievous letter to the Prince of Wales sent in 1798, to note that, 'as for General Garth, the purple light of love *toujours le méme*,' but on the subject of his connection with Princess Sophia, 'that is too near to make any observations upon.'[4]

And what exactly was that connection?

Despite Mary's comments on Garth's birthmark, let's not forget that good looks are far from everything. Garth was urbane and well-travelled, confident and successful. For a young lady who was starved of male company, it's not hard to imagine that Sophia might have developed a bit of a crush on this man of the world who was such an integral part of the household. Diarist Charles Greville certainly didn't doubt it and he wrote gleefully that the daughter of one of the queen's ladies-in-waiting had confided to him that the young princess was 'so in love with [Garth] that everyone saw it. She could not contain herself in his presence.' It wasn't any old lady-in-waiting either but Elizabeth Thynne, Marchioness of Bath and the queen's Mistress of the Robes. Few were closer to Queen Charlotte than she was.

These rumours of a secret love soon grew into more and when Princess Sophia was spirited off to Weymouth for an extended period in 1800 with some unexplained and mysterious malady, there was one word on the lips of court gossips.

Pregnancy.

But before we get to the child – for there certainly *was* a child, even if we can't be sure who the parents were – let's try and work out where the rumours began.

The marriage of Princess Sophia's beloved brother, the Prince of Wales, and his wife, Caroline, was ill-fated from the off. Wales was already married for one thing and had agreed to the official union only so that he might have his debts settled as part of the agreement. Caroline, meanwhile, was ill-suited to her fastidious, selfish husband. At their very first meeting, they disliked one another on sight.

Although they somehow managed to have a child together, within twelve months of their wedding the Prince and Princess of Wales were irretrievably estranged. Caroline went to live in Blackheath, where her husband's political opponents beat a path to her door and soon, so rumour had it, they were beating a path to her bed too. Wales spent the next two decades tearing his hair out and searching for a way to escape his marriage. In the event he only did so when Caroline died. In the late 1700s, she was still very much alive.

Sophia's friend, Frances Garth, was Caroline's woman of the bedchamber at Blackheath. Wales had no idea that Sophia and Frances had remained friends on her departure but in fact they were exchanging secret letters via intermediaries. What those letters contained we can't say but if Caroline got wind of the fact that there was an intrigue between Thomas Garth and Sophia via his niece, it's not impossible to think that she might have whipped up the rumours just to cause embarrassment to the Prince of Wales. Sophia, however, was rather fond of Caroline too so might we look a little closer to home for the source of the rumours? Did Wales, capricious, hot-tempered and not immune to spite, have it in himself to attack his own sister with gossip? Undoubtedly. The fact that Sophia was close to Caroline would have been motive enough.

Sophia was taken mysteriously ill in 1800 and disappeared from the already limited public outings she took, spending much of the year secluded at Weymouth. In 1801 her sister, Princess Elizabeth, approached one of the king's doctors, Thomas Willis, and asked if she could speak to him on 'a very delicate subject' that turned out to be 'the cruelty of a fabricated and most scandalous and base report concerning P.S. [Princess Sophia].' Willis committed nothing of their conversation to paper but was quick to note that there could be no truth whatsoever in the rumour that concerned Princess Sophia. The rumour was, of course, that Sophia's seclusion in Weymouth had been intended to conceal an unwanted pregnancy.

Princess Sophia and Thomas Garth had been at Windsor Castle together during the winter of 1799 when a prolonged illness forced her to move out of the draughty Lower Lodge and into the Upper Lodge.

This was the residence of the king and queen, who were away in London at the time. It was also the residence of Thomas Garth during his periods on duty and he was entrusted with the care of the princess, however you want to interpret that. If there *was* an affair and I believe that there probably was, this is where it began. This is certainly likely to be the period in which the rumoured child was conceived.

As the months passed, Sophia began to pile on weight until even her sickly father noticed the change in her physique. Fearing that any mention of a possible pregnancy might tip him back into madness, Queen Charlotte told George that the princess was ill with dropsy and the side effects of too much roast beef. She would soon be well again, Charlotte promised, and the excess weight would fall off.

Nine months later, Sophia was in Weymouth under the care of her physician, Sir Francis Milman. If Lady Bath was to be believed, then Sophia gave birth to a son in early August 1800. On 5 August the baptism of a founding tellingly named Thomas was recorded in the parish records. This little *foundling* was entrusted to the care of a local tailor and his wife, Samuel and Charlotte Sharland, but the gossip didn't stop there. When little Tommy was delivered to the Sharlands, who knew nothing of his origins, he was swaddled in an ornate silk skirt which bore an embroidered coronet, suggesting he was from anything but humble stock. All the arrangements for his care and the cost of his upkeep were to be made by Thomas Garth on the understanding that the couple would keep the details to themselves.

They didn't, of course.

Instead the Sharlands were fascinated by the mysterious child and his distinguished guardian. Whatever Tommy needed, Garth paid for and soon the living standards of the Sharlands were on the up. The couple began to ask too many questions about the mother and father of their so-called *foundling* and Garth pulled the plug. He took Tommy out of the Sharland household and gave him to the care of Major Herbert Taylor, then private secretary to the Duke of York. There he remained until 1804, when Thomas Garth adopted the boy who shared his name and began to raise him as his own. Nobody doubted that he was the child's real father, but the name of his real mother was never spoken except by gossips.

One of those gossips was Lord Glenbervie, a good friend of Caroline of Brunswick, the mischief-making Princess of Wales.

During a supposedly well-meaning discussion with Glenbervie, Caroline speculated whether it was likely that Sophia simply hadn't realised she was pregnant until she was virtually in labour. It might sound odd to us, but Caroline concluded that it wouldn't be so strange at all. It was possible, she and Glenbervie agreed, that Sophia 'did not perceive something particular had passed, and [she might] think it [sexual intercourse] a matter as indifferent and as unlikely to have consequences as blowing her nose.'[5]

Sophia was sheltered, after all, and her regular battles with ill health might have led her to miss all the obvious symptoms of pregnancy or to dismiss them as something else. If all of this is true though, the fact that Garth's career in the royal household continued is intriguing, for one might expect him to have been paid off and settled somewhere suitably genteel and safely out of the way. Instead he remained in the royal inner circle, eventually entrusted with the care of Princess Charlotte of Wales by her father. Of course, if Wales was aware that Garth and Sophia had a child, perhaps what tipped the balance in his favour was the fact that Garth assumed responsibility for the boy and, crucially, never whispered so much of a word about Sophia's reputation. If that was the case, then he had shown himself to be loyal beyond the point of questioning. Who better to trust with his daughter than the man who could have ruined a princess and yet said nothing, instead weathering the gossip with squared shoulders and stoic silence?

Glenbervie certainly believed that 'the foundling [is] now admitted by the people about the Court to be the Princess Sophia's, and, as the story generally goes, by General Garth.' I believe that Glenbervie was right and so it seems did most of the court, except one man who remained in the dark. Whilst Glenbervie was sure that 'the Queen knows the child to be the Princess Sophia's, [the] king does not.'[6]

Sophia, meanwhile, knew precisely what people were saying about her. With an almost audible sigh she lamented in a letter to Lady Harcourt that 'I must bear the reports, however unjust they are, as I have partially myself to thank for them... It is grievous to think what *a little trifle will slur a young woman's character for ever* [sic].' Though the exact meaning of this letter can only be open to conjecture, if Sophia had gushed of her attraction and perhaps even a liaison with Garth to his niece, Frances, then it's easy to see why she might have believed herself to be partially to blame for the rumours. Less easy to interpret, however, is her reference to a 'a little trifle', as surely Princess Sophia would know that an illegitimate child was far more than a trifle?

Unless Glenbervie's assertion below is true.

> '[As] the King has told [the princesses] he would never permit any of them to marry, they may indulge themselves in the gratifications of matrimony, if they manage matters with prudence and decorum, and form attachments as near to conjugal connection as the restriction imposed on them will admit of.'[7]

If this was the case, it's certainly borne out by other rumours regarding the princess, including some that she had entered into a secret marriage with Garth. She wore a ring that he gave her and though it was true that such a marriage wouldn't be legally recognised thanks to the Royal Marriages Act, in Sophia's mind it would certainly be binding in the eyes of God. A child born within marriage might seem more of a trifle than one born outside of wedlock but still 'a little trifle' seems too flippant for a woman of Sophia's intelligence and sensitivity. On the other hand, had her relationship with Garth been nothing more than a crush and maybe some harmless flirting then a trifle would be on the money. I don't believe that though, but I do wonder if she was doing her best to throw Lady Harcourt off the scent and make her believe that there had been nothing more scandalous behind the rumours than a young woman's innocent fancy.

Garth made no secret of his attachment to Tommy and could often be seen with him enjoying the Weymouth seafront whenever members of the royal household visited. The little boy was educated at Harrow and went onto a military career and some scandal of his own, as we shall learn later, but if the relationship between Garth and Princess Sophia survived Tommy's birth, by 1805 it was over. By that point Sophia, who was then in her late twenties, had declared that she would never visit Weymouth again, so terrified was she of meeting with some unnamed *something*. It's likely that what she feared was coming face to face with little Tommy Garth.

All Sophia wanted was to move on.

But I promised you that we'd get to Cumberland, so let us now delve into a *very* dark rumour.

Brotherly Affection

'Dear Ernest is as kind to me as it is possible, rather a little
imprudent at times, but when told of it never takes ill.'

And with these lines, the Duke of Cumberland's reputation faced
the first of what was to become a whole shopping list of villainous
accusations. From rape to incest to murder, he was the ogre of the
family and his undeserved reputation as a monster has followed him
ever since.

Prince Ernest Augustus, Duke of Cumberland, was the fifth son of
Charlotte and George and he later became the king of Hanover who,
you may recall, waged war on Queen Victoria in pursuit of his late
mother's diamonds. Cumberland had seen military service at the sharp
end which had left him partially blind and facially disfigured. Should
you ever see a portrait of Cumberland painted after the mid-1790s
you'll notice that he always favoured his right side, as the scarring was
on the left. Sometimes artists simply depicted Cumberland without any
scars at all. Crass though it may be, these battle scars did nothing to
improve his reputation and his hard-line political stance hardly helped
matters either.

When Sophia mentioned Cumberland's *imprudence*, it's more than
likely that she was referring to his troublemaking ways. However, when
rumours regarding a mysterious baby began to emerge, *imprudence* took
on a whole new meaning for some.

'The Duke of Kent tells the Princess [of Wales] that the father is not
Garth but the Duke of Cumberland. How horrid,'[8] wrote Lord Glenbervie
with scarcely concealed glee at the sheer amount of muck he and the
understandably embittered Caroline of Brunswick were able to rake up
over this particular matter. The Duke of Kent's involvement is frankly
difficult to swallow. One can hardly imagine him whispering such
potentially ruinous family secrets into the ear of Caroline of Brunswick,
the estranged wife of his brother and a woman who *loved* to tell stories.
Besides, Kent and Sophia had no quarrel and he had no reason to share
such bizarre tales with anyone.

Cumberland's sometimes inscrutable behaviour didn't help. Frances
Burney recalled the following incident, which hardly casts him in a

favourable light. She presents him as a skulking, peeping shadow, and an odd fellow indeed.

> 'A door was now opened from an inner apartment, where, I believe, was the grand collation for the Princess Sophia's birthday, and a tall thin young man appeared at it, peeping and staring, but not entering.
> 'How do you do, Ernest?' cried the Princess [Augusta]; 'I hope you are well; only pray do shut the door.' He did not obey, nor move, either forwards or backwards, but kept peering and peeping. She called to him again, beseeching him to shut the door; but he was determined to first gratify his curiosity, and when he had looked as long as he thought pleasant, he entered the apartment.'[9]

Cumberland was far from an easy fellow to know but with Sophia he was always friendly and attentive. *Too friendly and attentive*, some had said, with diarist Elizabeth Ham commenting on an occasion when the royal family were disembarking from a boat and Cumberland 'darted into the boat, seized on the Princess Sophia and kissed her'[10], but this is hardly the sort of evidence we can use to try a man for the rape of his own sister.

The accusation that dogged Cumberland can't go unremarked in these pages though, because it certainly isn't a new one. Thanks to the Georgian gossip mill, it was doing the rounds at the same time as little Tommy Garth was starting out on his new life. If Sophia heard of it, she must have been horrified.

Personally, I don't believe it for a moment. Cumberland certainly wasn't a saint but there's no evidence beyond strained conjecture to suggest that he fathered Tommy. Thomas Garth, however, not only gave the boy his name but funded his upbringing, sent him to Harrow and raised him as his own. Garth was well-known and well-liked by Princess Sophia and the time they spent together at Windsor fits perfectly with the dates when Tommy would have been conceived and that's without any veiled references to 'the purple light of love'. Though the evidence that supports Garth being Tommy's father is circumstantial, there's plenty of it. Not so in the case of Cumberland. Likewise, if Tommy was conceived when Cumberland raped Sophia, to have placed the baby with an equerry so closely tied to the royal family would have made no sense at all, especially since it was bound to lead to rumours about Garth's part in Tommy's conception. In the unthinkable event that Tommy was the son of Sophia and Cumberland he would have been raised far, far away from the royal family's beloved Weymouth.

Tommy Garth would be back to make more trouble later but for now at least, he was safely in school and the gossip was fading. Sophia's little brush with scandal was over.

A Dutiful Daughter

Life didn't return to normal for Princess Sophia after the strange episode of Weymouth, for there was no longer anything normal about the royal household. Or if there was, normality was a king in crisis, his doctors powerless to cure him as he rambled and raved, his health failing a little more with every episode. George enjoyed Sophia's gentle company but spending prolonged periods of time with the king led to a repeat of her earlier bouts of ill health. This time there was no doubt that it was her nerves that were the cause of her suffering. With Queen Charlotte distancing herself from George, it was left to Sophia to provide him with a confidante and inevitably the strain began to tell. She was placed under further pressure by the expectation that she should provide Wales with bulletins of Princess Amelia's deteriorating condition. Her days were an unhappy and exhausting round of nursing and reporting which never seemed to end. Whilst Sophia was looking out for everyone else, nobody seemed to be looking out for her.

When the death of Princess Amelia left the king shattered beyond all medical help, Sophia felt the strain not only of Amelia's loss but her father's illness too. The state of Sophia's nerves can be ascertained from a letter written by Lady Albinia Cumberland in 1811. She had visited Windsor as an attendant to the princesses and described the state of the household in a letter to her daughter. Remember that Lady Albinia was just there temporarily. For Sophia, however, the king's outbursts were an everyday occurrence.

> 'The King remains in the same state, he has been worse but is now rather better again as to *bodily health*. The mind is

134

the same – constant talking, laughing, sometimes singing. His conversation for now a fortnight was with imaginary Beings or rather those that are dead – particularly Prince Octavius a Prince who died at 5 years of age and whom he doated [sic] on. [...] He appears always happy, except when it is necessary to oppose him in his wishes – then his rage is excessive.

[...]

I have been taking a long walk with the Princesses [...] Poor things! how I do pity them! But no one so much as Princess Sophia. She is quite broken hearted!'[11]

Trapped in the cloisters of what she called the nunnery, Sophia had taken on the role of carer to the king that Queen Charlotte refused to bear and in doing so, she came to resent her mother more than perhaps all the other princesses did. Loyal and loving to her father, it grieved her to see that her mother preferred to avoid him altogether. Instead she sent Sophia off to keep him company whilst she locked herself away, safely out of reach. Charlotte was a widow whose husband had yet to die.

The rumours of an illegitimate child had already ruined Sophia's chances of finding a husband, but even before that, her chances of marriage were slim anyway. As her anxiety worsened the spasms returned, and while some of the princesses grew fat, Sophia began to fade away. The once cheery and excitable princess grew frustrated and sickly as the years passed and her father succumbed to insanity.

Perhaps surprisingly, the Prince Regent was sensitive to the needs and sacrifices of his sisters in a way that their mother never was.

'Poor old wretches as we are, four old cats, four old wretches, a dead weight upon you, old lumber to the country, like old clothes,' Sophia wrote to her eldest brother with a wry, if regretful air. 'I wonder you do not vote for putting us in a sack and drowning us in the Thames. Two of us would be fine food for the fishes and as to Minny and me, we will take our chance together.'[12]

The Regent, as we've already seen, did no such thing. Instead he granted his sisters allowances, coaches, liveries and even their own establishments, but for Sophia the prolonged strain had proved too much. Whilst her sisters revelled in their new-found freedom, limited though it was, Sophia was still in her *nunnery*. She was confined mostly to her bed by those mysterious spasms until there were genuine fears for her life. Sophia was entrusted to the care of Sir Henry Halford, who watched over the princess as she finally turned the corner and began to recover. It was a long and slow process and this time there was no rumour of scandal. Princess Sophia was simply exhausted.

Leaving Windsor

> 'I got a very comfortable conversation with Bailly [the royal physician, who] told me he saw & could tell me there was no end to [Sophia's] illness; that it was endless, that hers & Amelia's sickness were *precisely the same*, tho' *not* originating from the *same* causes as Amelia's did; that they are always obliged to change her medicines from one day to another, as they disagree & do not remain in her stomach, & that having no digestion at all it is greatly to be feared she will sink under it, having so little strength. In short I left Windsor quite oppressed & unhappy about that amiable little being.'[13]

The words of Princess Charlotte of Wales, recalling as they did the diagnosis of her physician, Dr Matthew Baillie, paint a horribly grim picture of Sophia's condition as the years unspooled. She became a solitary and frail figure, absent from such sisterly outings as the visit to the State Opening of Parliament that had caused such a ruction with Queen Charlotte, and appearing in the society columns only when they reported that she was, once again, indisposed by illness.

Yet if Baillie feared that Sophia was also succumbing to the sickness that had plagued her youngster sister and curtailed her life, might there have been another fear? The king's own illness had started as a physical one and look where it had ended. Like her father, Sophia struggled with her nerves and just like him, she gradually disappeared from what little public visibility she had ever had. Sensitive and easily upset, it wasn't outside the realms of possibility that Sophia might have inherited her father's condition too. Dr Bailie, on the other hand, didn't think this was the case. As far as he was concerned, Sophia was depressed, *nervous* as he called it, and physically weak. There was no need to fear for her long-term mental health.

Sophia's perilous condition meant that she couldn't be with Queen Charlotte at the moment of her passing. Though she could no longer make the short walk to her father's quarters, Sophia still received daily bulletins on the state of his health, whilst Sir Henry Halford was sending similar reports on her own wellbeing to her brothers. They shared the late Princess Charlotte's opinion that they must prepare for Sophia 'not being long lived, both from her tender & dwindling state; besides wh[ich] her sensitive mind & exquisite feeling must have had too many death blows for her spirits or her hea[l]th ever to recover.'[14]

With the death of Queen Charlotte, the death knell seemed to sound for Sophia too. Royal wrote sadly to Lady Harcourt that 'poor, dear Sophia is so seriously ill, and I fear she will not long survive our mother.' In the event the ever-sickly, worryingly frail princess outlived almost all of her siblings, not to mention living for thirty years longer than Queen Charlotte, confounding all those who had predicted nothing for her but an early grave.

Instead Sophia endured, her health forever perilous, her nerves forever frayed, her horizons no wider than the gentle, short walks she allowed herself at Windsor in the company of her sisters. Her world was a twilight one but in 1820, when two deaths rocked what remained of the Windsor nunnery, Sophia was left with no choice but to pack her things and go. First came the unexpected passing of the Duke of Kent thanks to those wet boots that he refused to change. Then, hot on the heels of that, King George III died.

On the death of Queen Charlotte, Sophia inherited Windsor's Lower Lodge but she had no intention of living there. Instead the wilting, lilting invalid who seemed to be constantly hovering on the threshold of death left Windsor for the capital on 18 February 1820. So long had reports been made of Sophia's imminent demise that her move to London came as a shock to all. The princess who had been too unwell to even leave the grounds of Windsor for many years was ready for a change.

Upon her move to London, Sophia initially took up residence in Cambridge House as a guest of her brother Prince Adolphus, Duke of Cambridge, and later moved to Kensington Palace, where she remained for the rest of her days. Though *The Morning Chronicle* reported somewhat prematurely in March that Sophia's health 'which has been in a very indifferent state for some years, is not at all improved by her residence in town,'[15] it seemed that the gentlemen of the press might have spoken too soon.

Quite unexpectedly, at Cambridge House Sophia began to slowly flourish. She could be seen taking the air in Cambridge's carriage or on horseback and even took the occasional trip out to inspect the fashionable new building works in Russell Square, a twilit phantom no longer. Though Henry Halford continued to monitor her, Sophia welcomed her siblings and a small number of friends into her new home for tea and even hosted the occasional evening engagement. To most of the great and the good of London such events would be an everyday occurrence but for Sophia they were indicative of a new start, one that had come not a minute too soon.

Sophia didn't exactly embark on a social whirlwind, but she was more active than she had been in years. When Royal returned for her visit to the land of her birth, Sophia was able to receive her eldest sister, who had no doubt long been expecting to find an invalid or a coffin in place of her frail sibling.

But for Sophia, the past was about to come calling. Though she never made mention of the sad end of the story of Tommy Garth, he had no intention of fading away.

A Scandalous Elopement

General Garth thought he had raised Tommy Garth to have everything a boy could wish for, from a father figure to the finest education. He had even hobnobbed in the most illustrious circles thanks to the general's position as guardian to Princess Charlotte of Wales in the months before her marriage. The plain-speaking princess thought that Tommy had been rather too indulged. She scowled at the way he paraded around Weymouth as though *he* was the senior royal, not her. Perhaps he believed himself to be so.

The aging Garth doted on Tommy and it must have been a proud day indeed when the young man decided to follow his adoptive – supposedly – father into the army, but his career wasn't anywhere near as glittering.

Rather than devote his life to King and country as Garth had done, the spoiled little boy grew into a pleasure-seeking young man and where better to find pleasure than amongst the notorious Dashwoods of West Wycombe, once famed for their singular *Hellfire Club*? Tommy eloped with Lady Georgiana Astley, a Dashwood daughter who just happened to have been married to Sir Jacob Astley for a decade. She was mother to two children by her husband but when she met Tommy, she was smitten. When the couple ran away, Lady Astley swiftly found herself the subject of divorce proceedings, though her reputation was salvaged to some degree when it was proved that Sir Jacob was far from a saint himself. The public lapped up every twist and turn in the scandalous story of the elopement and it was splashed across the papers.

In the days before his death in 1829, General Garth supposedly gave Tommy a locked box containing several letters that would prove beyond a doubt *exactly* who his parents were. We might imagine, I think, that the evidence was in favour of Garth and Princess Sophia. By the time General Garth died, Tommy's lavish lifestyle had left him up to his eyeballs in debt and he wrote to Sophia to request a financial bailout. Whether she ever saw the letter or not, we don't know, but we *do* know that the matter was handed over to Tommy's short-lived former caretaker, Sir Herbert Taylor, by now Private Secretary to King George IV. According to popular legend, the letter Tommy sent was nothing short of blackmail, demanding cash in return for his silence. If no payment was forthcoming, he would have no alternative but to make the general's papers public.

A wily old operator with decades of experience behind him, Taylor made a counter-offer. If Tommy Garth deposited the locked box and all its contents safely in a bank, Taylor would see to it that he would be rewarded with a generous yearly salary of £3,000. Tommy was quick to agree. He kept his side of the bargain and deposited his blackmail box. As soon as he did so, it promptly disappeared without a trace, never to be seen again. Tommy was livid and issued an affidavit against Sir Herbert Taylor demanding the return of the box and its contents. Naturally the press went to town, unpicking the threads of scandal and trying to find out where the tantalising path might lead.

It led, surprise, surprise to the oft-maligned Cumberland, and Tommy now claimed that the box contained letters from Sophia in which she accused her brother of attempted rape. Though they daren't go so far as to explicitly publish Tommy's accusations, the gentlemen of the Georgian press were masters of insinuation. Any reader, said *The Morning Post*, would 'recoil with horror at [Tommy Garth's] unmanly and dishonourable conduct, and blush crimson deep with shame at their own credulity in giving currency to the foulest insinuations against the

Duke of CUMBERLAND, who, we openly and authorizedly state, is as free from even the suspicion of any criminal knowledge of Captain GARTH's birth or circumstances as the child unborn.'[16]

Tommy was no gentleman of honour, concluded the press, but a man who had lived beyond his means and now sought to rectify that by demanding money from innocent royals. While this unseemly public business was being played out, General Thomas Garth died. In his will, he left bequests to family members including his niece, Frances, who had been Princess Sophia's friend, and one to his son, Tommy. Of the princess, of course, there was no mention.

By the time Garth died on 18 November 1829, his son's debts had caught up with him and he was flung into debtors' prison. Loyal to the last, Georgiana went with him and she gave birth to their only child, Georgiana Rosamond, behind bars. Soon afterwards Lady Georgiana died, leaving her lover to raise their child in what might have been dire straits if not for the intervention of Sir Herbert Taylor.

Unsurprisingly, it was Taylor who eventually pulled the strings that shut down the scandal. By the time he did, Tommy had been in prison for five long years. Taylor conjured up a lump sum of £10,000 from the estate of the late General Garth and was able to secure the release of Tommy and his little girl. The salary of £3,000 that Tommy had demanded never materialised, but Taylor did agree to an annuity of £300. Apart from the occasional libel suit against the newspapers that had covered the strange story of the locked box, the scandal had fizzled out. Tommy Garth, at last, faded into obscurity.[17]

Aunt Sophia

Whilst Taylor and Tommy worked out their delicate negotiation, Princess Sophia continued what had become a serene existence. Safely ensconced in her apartments in Kensington Palace she devoted her time and energy to her niece, Victoria, and when George IV died in 1830, she needed the cheerful company of the little girl more than ever. By now approaching old age, Sophia was partially deaf and struggling with her eyesight.

> 'Gossips sought in vain for hereditary insanity in this large family. None of George III's fifteen children were mad, but many had indifferent sight. Princess Sophia was quite blind.'[18]

140

Always a martyr to her health, Sophia suddenly lost the use of her right eye to a cataract in 1832. By now well-used to dealing with such drama, she chalked it up to age and got on with living. But her dramas weren't done yet and her precious relationship with Princess Victoria wasn't plain sailing either. For that we have the notorious Sir John Conroy to thank.

As comptroller (head of the household) and very likely lover to Victoria's ambitious widowed mother, the Duchess of Kent, Conroy had his sights set on the highest of prizes. It was he who masterminded the restrictive and isolating Kensington System under which Victoria was brought up, subject to the constant watch and discipline of her strict mother. The system was intended to weaken the young princess' resolve and leave her open to manipulation. Conroy was certain that the aging King William IV wouldn't live long enough for Victoria to reach her majority and that would mean a Regent must be appointed. In his grand plan, he foresaw that the Regent would be the Duchess of Kent, a puppet ruler with her comptroller pulling the strings.

Victoria saw through Conroy's schemes and proved to be more than able to resist even his fiercest attempts to control her. Yet Conroy, manipulative, ambitious and charming, saw in the elderly and vulnerable Princess Sophia a person who he could easily bend to his will. She came to support him in his disagreements with Victoria and eventually became his informant, reporting on the young woman's comings and goings whenever Conroy was away. Princess Sophia gave Conroy complete control of her finances and he went to town. Whilst she lived a parsimonious lifestyle, Conroy's life was one of luxury and opulence, most of it paid for by the unwitting Sophia. In fact, when she died in 1848, she had less than £2,000 to her name. Conroy, meanwhile, was living like a king.

Sophia was dealt a painful blow in 1838 when she lost the sight in her healthy left eye after submitting to an operation that she hoped might safely remove another cataract. The operation failed, rendering her totally blind. Though she now required the help of attendants to carry out even the simplest tasks, her remaining siblings rallied round her, keen to stave off any melancholy she might feel. For more than a decade Sophia's life was one of infirmity, but she was never without friendly company in her dotage.

To the end of her days, Sophia was an elder stateswoman of an adoring royal family. When the once-reclusive Princess took her last breath on 27 May 1848 at York House, she was surrounded by members of her family.

> 'Her Royal Highness the Princess Sophia, daughter of his late Majesty George III., and aunt to the Queen, expired at half-past six o'clock on Saturday afternoon, at her residence at Kensington.
>
> The Princess became very ill on Saturday morning, and was visited by her royal sister the Duchess of Gloucester, who returned in the afternoon. Her Majesty the Queen Dowager, and his Royal Highness Prince Albert paid visits in the course of the day.
>
> Later in the afternoon, the Duchess of Kent, the Duchess of Gloucester, and the Duchess of Cambridge, assembled at the Princess's residence, and were with her royal highness when she expired. The Duchess of Inverness was also present at the period of the melancholy event. The Duke of Cambridge arrived a few minutes after his royal sister had breathed her last.'[19]

With the death of Sophia, Mary alone remained of those daughters of George III. Of fifteen children, now there were but three: the Duke of Cambridge, the King of Hanover and the Duchess of Gloucester. Sophia was laid to rest beside her brother, Augustus, at Kensal Green Cemetery according to her own wishes. It was perhaps an odd choice for a princess whose family usually chose Windsor as their resting place but Sophia, reclusive, placid and watchful, was never what one might call predictable. She'd spent long enough at Windsor for one lifetime.

Act Seven

Princess Amelia of the United Kingdom (7 August 1783 – 2 November 1810)

The Last Daughter

And so, after illegitimate children, secret marriages and the confines of the *nunnery*, we finally come to the last of the six daughters of George III and Charlotte of Mecklenburg-Strelitz. She was Princess Amelia, *the sickly one*. Or to be more correct, *another* sickly one.

There were lots of *sickly ones* among the daughters of George and Charlotte, but none had a life that was quite so characterised by illness as Amelia. She spent most of her short life languishing and longing. Exactly *who* she was longing for we shall soon discover, but it shouldn't come as any surprise to learn that it was unfulfilled. There was a full seventeen years between the birth of the eldest royal daughter and the youngest and in recognition of their status, Royal and Augusta were to serve as the baby's godmothers. With Amelia's birth, Queen Charlotte's childbearing days finally came to an end. What a sigh of relief she and her body must have breathed.

Princess Amelia, known to her family as *Emily*, was born into a household in mourning. The twin tragedies of Alfred and Octavius' deaths had left a pall over the royal family that chilled the once happy home. For the king, this new daughter was a gift from God, a ray of sunlight in an iron grey sky and he loved her above all his other surviving children. Whether his adoration for her surpassed his devotion to the late Octavius is debateable but it certainly equalled it, at the very least. So great was his love for Amelia that her death, when it came, shattered what little remained of his tenuous grip on reality. At first though, the birth of the new princess was like a breaking dawn and when the Treaty of Paris officially ended the American War of Independence just a month later, George III looked ahead to a new start. Grief and conflict were over. He had a delightful new daughter to get to know.

If only.

Amelia was a very young child when the king experienced his first prolonged bout of insanity, but very young children have a sixth sense for family trouble. Like *Minny*, she must have been aware of the unhappy atmosphere that settled over her home, the unspoken stress and tension, not to mention the distraction of her mother and the sudden disappearance of her loving, engaged father from her life. You might recall Mary, *little Minny*, pining for the king and constantly fretting about him as she peered through windows and wondered when he would return. You might also recall the failed and ill-conceived experiment when Mary and Amelia were held up to see their father as he walked in the garden. Far from being delighted at the sight, the king threw down his hat and cane and fled, hysterical, for the safety of Kew.

How Amelia would have wondered not only at the king's absence, but also at the shadow of a man she saw taking the air, teary and confused. She must have felt a chill at the king's uncanny, seemingly endless laughter as it echoed around the draughty corridors like that of a phantom.

As if that weren't troubling enough, Dr Willis decided that the best thing for his patient's health would be to bring Amelia into the king's company, in the belief that her presence would cause George to become calmer. The monarch certainly tried to check himself but still he ranted and garbled, giving the young princess a weirdly prescient, detailed and blow-by-blow account of the circumstances and order of service of her own funeral. Through all of this, the attendants were constantly poised, ready to swoop in and sweep Amelia away from the king if his behaviour was believed to pose a threat to her. It didn't, but what an odd impression this must have made on the little girl.

Yet if Amelia had any reservations about her father's twilight existence and surely she must have done, none of it did anything to lessen her pleasant nature. She was bright and bubbly, inquisitive and happy and it's very easy to see why the king settled so much affection on her. Amelia was a child still, a world away from the Princess Royal and her agitation for freedom, and in her George could enjoy the same carefree silliness and unconditional love that he had once known from Octavius and Alfred, the children who were so cruelly taken from him. She asked for nothing from her father but his love, her innocence and youth leaving her unable to understand his problems or worry about what they might mean for her prospects longer term, even without the ruinous illness that eventually consumed her.

The king's illness meant that Princess Amelia's education was less stringent than that of her sisters. With Queen Charlotte's attention focussed on George, it was left for the Princess Royal to supervise her youngest sister. She did so with her customary care and attention, but perhaps without Charlotte's rigid and unswerving routine. Of course, Amelia didn't care. She was the favourite of the king and she adored him in her turn. What need did she have for education when George was waiting to lavish her with adoration? It's notable that her first official public appearance was in 1789, when she joined her sisters to take part in the procession of thanksgiving for the king's recovery at St Paul's. It's notable too that during one of the reunions between the king and Amelia, George became so excited at the sight of her that he swore that he and Amelia would never be parted from that day forward. It was a promise that he couldn't keep, no matter how hard he tried.

The First Symptoms

For most of her youth, Princess Amelia showed no sign of significant illness, and certainly never experienced anything that would confine her to bed. In a group of daughters who had progressively become frailer, she was comparatively healthy, but that was all ended in 1798 when quite out of nowhere the princess complained of a pain in her knee. A fine horsewoman who was usually in the highest spirits possible, the agonising swelling came on without warning and crippled her. Though her family took their usual sojourn to Weymouth, Amelia and Lady Albinia Cumberland were packed off to Worthing instead. The journey was much shorter than that her family was undertaking but it was hoped that she'd be able to reap the benefits of sea bathing and fresh air. Sadly, that hope was to prove false. The tuberculosis in Princess Amelia's knee did not improve.

Despite the attentive care of physician Sir Lucas Pepys and surgeon Thomas Keate, Amelia's health grew weaker and weaker. She suffered through an agonising treatment programme involving electrification, leeches and of course plenty of bloodletting, alternating with long periods of rest with occasional forays on horseback to keep her knee from seizing up. Amelia was in constant agony yet to the outside world, she was the picture of robust womanhood. It's easy to read her story and picture a frail, waiflike creature hovering between life and death, but the princess was able and strong and frustrated by her own immobility. Though Sophia was ethereal, Amelia looked to be on track to share the build of her eldest sister. This made her sudden and unexpected descent into illness even more difficult for her family to deal with.

When Amelia returned from Worthing, she went to stay for a time with Sir Lucas Pepys and his family at Juniper Hill. Pepys and Keate decided that she was well enough to receive a visit from the old family retainer. In fact, they said with pride, the treatments were succeeding. Amelia was on the mend.

Burney painted an initial picture not of a swooning invalid, but of Princess Amelia 'seated on a sofa, in a French gray riding-dress, with pink lapels, her beautiful and richly flowing and shining fair locks unornamented. [She] received me with the brightest smile, calling me up to her, and stopping my profound reverence, by pouting out her sweet ruby lips for me to kiss.'[1] Yet at the end of the meeting the true extent of her disability became apparent. Once a sprightly and healthy horsewoman, as Burney watched she was 'painfully lifted from her seat between Sir Lucas and Mr Keate.'[2] Despite her obvious struggles, Amelia's physicians declared that all of that bloodletting and electrification had been a success – their patient was on the road to recovery.

In fact, Princess Amelia would never be truly well again.

The Attentive Equerry

At last it seemed as though the worst was over. Amelia was once again seen riding her beloved horses with confidence and the year after her trip to Worthing she was back in Weymouth, enjoying or perhaps enduring the regular royal holiday. If any of the princesses was giving cause for concern it was Sophia, weak and unwell as she was to be throughout her life even as her younger sister's recovery continued apace.

It couldn't last.

In 1801 the king complained that he was feeling unwell and, just like that, the symptoms that had brought such misery to Windsor years earlier returned. Once again, the fearsome doctors were summoned and once again, George III lost control of his faculties. This time the episode was brief and George was able to take his usual summer sojourn to Windsor but even as the king recovered, his youngest daughter was sliding in the other direction. When the trip to Weymouth reached its conclusion, it was decided that Amelia should remain behind at the resort for a few days so she might continue to benefit from the sea air. Here she was joined by the erstwhile Jane Gomm and Charles FitzRoy, the king's equerry. Not just any old equerry though, but an equerry who could trace his lineage all the way back to none other than Charles II and his mistress, Barbara Villiers.

Is all of this starting to sound familiar? If you're thinking of Brent Spencer, in some ways you'd be right to do so but apart from the central conceit of a princess and an equerry, the sophisticated FitzRoy and the rather more eccentric Spencer had precious little in common. If your mind went straight to Thomas Garth, however, there may be something to be said for that. But whilst the princesses could make snide asides about Garth's birthmark, for FitzRoy there was to be no such mockery.

Charles FitzRoy was the second son of Baron Southampton and at twenty-one years older than Princess Amelia, he had already enjoyed a long and successful army career. Like Garth and Spencer, he too was one of the king's most trusted and loyal equerries, and a man for whom George III felt real affection. So well-loved was he by the sovereign that the courtiers even nicknamed him *Prince* Charles. Urbane, handsome and experienced, FitzRoy had impressed no less a monarch than Frederick the Great during a sojourn in Germany as a young man. He was the ideal chap to care for Princess Amelia during her extended trip to the seaside.

Just as Amelia was an experienced and accomplished horsewoman, so FitzRoy was more than her equal. There was nothing the princess liked more than to deliberately drop back in the party so that she might ride beside the man who had become her favourite equerry. This continued upon her return to Windsor, when King George would ride at the head of the party with FitzRoy and Amelia tagging along behind. When night fell and card games occupied the evening, Amelia and FitzRoy made sure to always be partnered together. It wasn't long before Mary noticed that Amelia had a favourite.

You will recall the upset when Mary discussed with Miss Gomm the concerns she had over what she believed was an entirely inappropriate relationship between a princess and an equerry. Having already tried to warn Amelia off FitzRoy, Miss Gomm shared her concerns with Princess Mary who, you may remember, spoke to Gouly. So hard of hearing was Gouly, according to Frances Burney, 'there is no talking with her, but by talking for a whole house to hear.' Yet despite the argument that took place between Mary and Amelia over her indiscreetly discussing such a private matter with the ladies of the household, Amelia must have known that there could only be worse to come if Queen Charlotte discovered her burgeoning relationship with the equerry. Indeed, when Queen Charlotte wrote to Amelia and warned her about 'riding near the King, and not to keep behind,' it seemed that the cat was very much out of the bag.

In 1803, Miss Gomm told the queen about FitzRoy and Amelia. What's interesting about Charlotte's reaction is how entirely unexpected it was. Rather than going through the roof as one might predict, she dealt with the issue with unexpected calm and discretion. Perhaps Charlotte simply thought that Miss Gomm was mistaken, or that FitzRoy was merely indulging the harmless whims of the young and bored princess, but she certainly didn't appear to be too furious when she wrote to Amelia about the situation. In fact, she didn't touch on the matter of FitzRoy at all, only on the argument between the sisters and the governess.

> '[Miss Gomm's job] is to put you upon your Guard, if she knows of anything that could be likely to injure you, and as she has seen much of the World knows by experience that the Higher the Rank in Life, the more the world expose them, because the World expects more circumspection in their conduct. She spoke to you only and there left it.'[3]

Charlotte went on to assure Amelia that Mary had sworn that none of her sisters knew of the gossip or the argument. She suggested that it might be a good idea to let the matter rest there. It seems that Amelia had taken affront at the comments regarding falling behind whilst out on rides and asked instead if she could be excused from riding altogether. On this point, Charlotte was immovable. Amelia must ride for her health, she said, and should she hear any mention of Amelia voicing her complaints to the king, there would be serious trouble. Charlotte was always very quick to bring her husband into arguments when she was looking for an easy win and this was no different. Drama would upset the patient, she warned, and upsetting the patient would be the worst thing that anyone could do. She closed with a plea for her daughter to take note of what she had said if not for the sake of a happy home, then for the sake of Amelia's precarious health. Too much upset, warned Queen Charlotte, might prove dangerous to one so unwell.

Amelia never trusted Gouly or Gomm again. To Mary, who was to become her loyal nurse, she extended a hand of truce. For now, at least.

FitzRoy, meanwhile, was all too aware of the gossip at court. In a letter the princess wrote to him we can see clues that his manner was as cool and detached as hers was passionate and that he, as the older of the couple, exerted an emotional pull over Amelia that she was desperate to preserve. Though the letter below is undated, I think it's safe to assume it comes from an early period of the relationship, when Amelia, who was not yet 20, was desperately seeking the approval of her soldier.

> 'MY OWN DEAR ANGEL,
> I don't know why, but I felt so full that I was quite distressed at speaking to you […] I thought your manner to me still as if you had doubts about me. That dear smile to-day gave me such pleasure, but I think something I did annoyed you to-night. [When you go out] I tell you Honestly how jealous I am you don't know! and I dread your hating me.
> [...]
> My own dear love I am sure you love me as well as ever. If you can give me a kind look or word to-night pray do, and look for me to-morrow morning riding, don't leave me, do let us be, if we can, in comfort, but tell me your mind, and the truth. Don't send anything over to me till this evening, you dear Angel.
> [...]
> Promise, after you go to town for the Meeting of Parliament, you will sit for me for I long for my picture. I want to talk to you, for you are not well. I see you change colour very often. Don't trifle with my happiness, which you do by not attending to your health, as all my happiness and comfort depends on my own dear darling.
> [...]

Did you tell [the Prince of Wales] how wretched we both
are? I hoped yesterday, at latest last night, I should have
heard from you. I dare say you had not time, and, as you
wrote that precious note before you went, I ought to have
been satisfied, but that I never am, separate from you, dear
Angel.'[4]

We can see from Amelia's heated words that she, like her sisters, believed
that Wales was the man in whom to confide. He alone could soothe the
queen when she became agitated – witness his securing not only peace for
the sisters but even a little freedom in the face of Charlotte's rage – and
he knew what it was to be unable to love freely. In the case of Amelia and
FitzRoy though, even the Princes of Wales was powerless to help.

A Fall

Though Amelia appeared to have overcome the tuberculosis in her knee,
her health remained turbulent. In 1803, the year in which the gossip
regarding FitzRoy became the talk of the ladies, she fell ill again. The man
appointed by the king to watch over her in her hour of need was none other
than Charles FitzRoy and we can imagine that he did so with aplomb. In
the company of her paramour the princess slowly began to recover and by
1804 she was well enough to join the family on their trips away. It's not
hard to imagine that some of her indisposition might have been down to her
fretting over FitzRoy. What a tonic it must have been to have him so near.

After her rebuke from Queen Charlotte for falling behind during
her rides Princess Amelia lost her appetite for horsemanship. Yet her
doctors decreed that she must ride for her health, so ride she did. The
princess was a more than proficient horsewoman but even the most
experienced equestrienne can take a tumble and in 1804 that's exactly
what happened. During a family trip to Southampton she was out riding
with her father when her horse threw her. George Rose, a politician and
friend of the king who was hosting the royal party, described the scene
and its aftermath.

'Of Lord North his Majesty was beginning to speak in
very favourable terms, when we were interrupted by the

Princess Amelia (who, with the other Princesses, was riding behind us) getting a most unfortunate fall. The horse, on cantering down an inconsiderable hill, came on his head, and threw her Royal Highness flat on her face. She rose, without any appearance of being at all hurt, but evidently a good deal shaken; and notwithstanding an earnest wish to avoid occasioning the slightest alarm, was herself not desirous of getting on horseback again; but the King insisted that she should, if at all hurt, get into one of the carriages and return to Cuffnells to be bled, or otherwise mount another horse and ride on. She chose the latter, and rode to Southampton, where she lost some blood unknown to the King. I hazarded an advice, that no one else would do, for her Royal Highness's return, which was certainly not well received, and provoked a quickness from his Majesty that I experienced in no other instance. He observed that he could not bear that any of his family should want courage. To which I replied, I hoped his majesty would excuse me if I said I thought a proper attention to prevent the ill effects of an accident that *had* happened, was no symptom of a want of courage. He then said with some warmth:- "Perhaps it may be so; but I thank God there is but one of my children who wants courage; - and I will not name HIM, *because he is to succeed me.*"[5]

There's obviously far more at play here than a father's unexpected reaction to what sounds like a nasty fall indeed. In the case of a fall like that experienced by Amelia, to pressure her into making a choice between continuing the ride and being bled is hardly much of a choice at all. Amelia knew from bitter experience how unpleasant it was to be bled. She'd rather take her chances in the saddle.

This was not the playful, silly king who had tumbled with his children on the castle rugs, this was the shadow of a man that the illness had left behind. Short of temper, filled with anxiety and sometimes sharp with even his favourite daughter, he was a changed character. Amelia also had the misfortune to experience her fall at a time when George was at dreadful odds with his eldest son and heir, the Prince of Wales. The king was under immense stress both personal and political and with it came the risk of a relapse into madness. Perhaps that explains why Amelia swallowed her pain and continued with the ride. Her father might dote on her, but even a doting father must be carefully managed.

Wife and Darling

Princess Amelia was devoted to the king and he to her and it's intriguing to note that her own health often seemed to grow weak at times of crisis for him too. She chided FitzRoy for making her ill by neglecting his own health and in Queen Charlotte's letters to her youngest daughter, there are frequent allusions to Amelia looking after herself properly and dark suggestions that anxiety and worry could only serve to make her sicklier still. Whether some of her ill health can be attributed to nerves can't really be satisfactorily established, but what *can* be established is that her devotion to the ailing George III never wavered. When her father was unwell, Amelia visited him, and they dined together at a table set just for the two of them. They were forming a court of their own.

The queen had grown more distant than ever from her husband and had taken to sleeping apart from him behind a locked door. She refused to travel alone with George and if she was to meet him anywhere, she insisted on having one of the princesses with her. This behaviour between the once adoring couple left her daughters unsettled. Amelia, like all her unmarried sisters, now knew without a doubt that a betrothal was unlikely. Instead of dreaming impossible dreams she contented herself with her not-so-secret love for FitzRoy and some historical rumour mongers have speculated that Amelia and the equerry undertook a secret marriage ceremony. Whether there was a ceremony or not, Amelia began to practise signing herself as AFR, in honour of FitzRoy.

Signatures can only entertain a young lady for so long and Princess Amelia was bored. She was bored with Weymouth, bored with her sisters, bored with the *nunnery*. Yet under the terms of the Royal Marriages Act we shouldn't doubt that Amelia knew she would never receive George's consent. All she could do – if she dared – was wait until she was 25 and make a request to the Privy Council for the permission to wed. As we'll learn, by the time that birthday rolled by, she was too unwell to do any such thing.

Amelia contented herself with riding and, like her sisters, with indulging her niece, Princess Charlotte of Wales. She watched as her contemporaries married and wrote wistfully to FitzRoy of how she envied them, growing ever more frustrated with the life she lived. In her letters, she bemoaned the queen's demeanour towards her and with Amelia and Mary ever at each other's side, scowled that Charlotte never wanted Mary to go anywhere, whereas 'to get rid of me is [Queen Charlotte's] object on every account.'. All she had was her attachment to FitzRoy, which she longed to make official.

> 'Pray don't alter in your manner to me in any thing, you dear Angel. I really must marry you, though inwardly united, and in reality that is much more than the ceremony, yet that ceremony would be a protection. O my precious darling, how often do I say – would to God my own husband and best friend and guardian was here. [...] Be assured of the unalterable attachment of your own for ever, your affectionate and devoted Wife and darling.'[6]

Amelia, the *wife and darling* who was practising to sign herself *AFR*, was filled with passion for her equerry. She made little effort to conceal it and in 1807 wrote to FitzRoy to inform him that a new rumour was doing the rounds. Once again Miss Gomm was gossiping, and this time she was in full soap opera mode, armed with anonymous letters that had been circulated at court regarding the intrigue. Miss Gomm told Princess Elizabeth that Amelia's honour was all but in tatters and that the queen had 'sanctioned the promise of a marriage the moment the K[ing] was dead.' This was, of course, nonsense. Charlotte was wed to protocol and would never agree to such a thing, for she had already decided that the girls belonged with her. Without her daughters, who else would she rail and complain at, after all?

When Queen Charlotte heard this new rumour, she reserved her fury not for her daughter, but for the gossips. To Amelia, she merely continued to stress the importance of prudence and morality, of piety over passion. Should she continue along her present course, Charlotte sighed, Amelia would make her father more ill than he had ever been. It was an unforgiveable and calculated accusation that Charlotte knew Amelia wouldn't be able to dismiss. She would never pursue her own happiness at the expense of her beloved father's health, even if he was too delusional to recognise that she had done any such thing.

Visits from Father

By 1807, Princess Amelia hardly knew where to turn. She had put all her trust in her attendant, Mrs George Villiers, and asked her to procure a copy of the Royal Marriages Act. Laid low by ill health, Amelia set about studying the Act. She longed to be married to FitzRoy and wrote that, 'for years I have considered myself his lawful wife', which doesn't quite put paid to speculation that there was a clandestine marriage of some sort. Amelia only *considered* herself his wife, but even with a secret ceremony, without adhering to the terms of the Royal Marriages Act, the union wouldn't be legal.

When Amelia wrote to the Prince of Wales that she would happily forego all her privileges and even her family if it were to mean that she could marry FitzRoy, she meant it. She truly believed that she could be happy only with him, but by now her health was in terminal decline. Though she little knew it, she wouldn't live to pursue her dream.

Princess Amelia's symptoms were further complicated by those of St Anthony's Fire, an agonising skin condition, but more worrying were the signs of fatal tuberculosis. She took to her bed once more with Mary at her beck and call. The queen kept her usual emotional distance and Amelia grew bitter towards her, coming to believe that Charlotte wished her to just get on and die and be done with it. Her letters took on a melancholy, fatalistic air, as though she had sensed her approaching death and was putting her affairs in good order before the moment came. Chief among them was her concern for FitzRoy's happiness after her passing. After loving him for ten long years, Amelia prepared a will in which she left FitzRoy virtually everything she possessed. To the man she called her *guide, protector, friend, husband, lover*, Amelia was beseeching. She begged him to seek a new life away from court and promised that even if she couldn't be beside him in the flesh, she'd be there in spirit instead.

Yet when she reached the age of 25, Amelia made no effort to seek the Privy Council's permission to marry. The reason for this isn't such a mystery, for though she'd told the Prince of Wales that she was considering it, in the event the threat of destroying her father's tenuous grip on reality must have proved too great. Queen Charlotte said no more on the matter and perhaps thought it finished but her disapproval was expressed in other ways. As Amelia languished, subject to repeated debilitating treatments of cupping and blistering by her physician, Sir Francis Milman, her mother was nowhere to be seen. Instead Amelia was left to her own devices and isolated for the supposed good of her health. All it did was give her time to brood. Amelia knew that she was making no progress and wrote to her mother – there was no other way to make contact – asking if there was a chance that she could have a second opinion and perhaps a different course of treatment. Charlotte was reluctant to consider it but ultimately Dr Pope was added to the gaggle of physicians at the princess' bedside. He was Amelia's preferred choice but Milman, Queen Charlotte's favourite, was never far away.

The learned doctors subjected Amelia to an intensive programme of agonising treatment. They dotted leeches around her face and body, cupped her and bled her and when all else failed, got out the seatons. When Amelia complained of terrible pains shooting through her side, the seaton was expected to give her some relief. Seatons were essentially tubes, initially made of silk and later of rubber, that were inserted into a hole in the patient's body and through which fluids could be drawn and discarded. In Amelia's case they didn't work. Instead they became embedded in Amelia's skin and Mary Gaskoin, her maid and friend, had to apply caustic to the princess' body to release the stuck seatons. The agony must have been indescribable but when Amelia wrote to her father, she spared him any details, admitting only that 'of course it was very painful & I have not had a good night.' One imagines that was an understatement.[7]

Princess Augusta gave her sister a songbird as a gift to keep her company and the family waited for the worst to happen. As well as Mary's attentive nursing, Amelia received visits from her siblings and her father, who was by now virtually blind. He had never ceased to adore his youngest daughter and received multiple daily bulletins regarding her condition, hoping desperately for any sign of recovery. Each afternoon the sovereign and his attendants hobbled down to see Amelia, frequently being brought to tears by her plight. Together father and daughter ruminated on faith and religion, each quietly preparing for their own expected demise. She received visits of a more clandestine nature from FitzRoy himself who, with the help of Princess Mary, was able to spend some precious time with his beloved in the last months of her short life.

The End of the Princess

By 1810 Princess Amelia, once a robust, healthy young woman, was gone. In her place at Augusta Lodge was a painfully thin phantom, bedbound, helpless and devoid of any hope of recovery. One can't help but admire the fortitude of the princess who accepted her inevitable demise with a strength of character that would shame many. She had undertaken one last trip to Weymouth in 1809 in the hope of finding a miracle cure but by that point, everyone knew that the princess had reached the point of no return. Carried to and from the sea in a specially constructed bathing machine, Amelia couldn't even bear the gentle lap of the waves without experiencing sickness. The very therapy that it was hoped might bring her comfort was instead leaving her ready to swoon away.

Aware that time was growing short, Amelia commissioned a ring which she wanted to give George as a memorial gift. The ring was decorated with diamonds and contained a lock of the princess' hair. It was inscribed with her name and the words, *remember me*. The ring was prepared with all haste by a jeweller who was well aware that he was racing against the clock and when it arrived, Amelia was determined to give it to George herself, but Princess Mary begged her to reconsider. She believed that giving their father the ring would leave him in turmoil, but Amelia was determined to have her way in this final gesture. It became one of the most poignant episodes in the life of King George III.

As ever, George made his daily visit to his daughter's bedside and took her frail hand in his. As he did, Amelia slipped the ring onto his finger and asked him to promise that he'd never forget her. George III, blind, sometimes incoherent and hallucinating, told her through his sobs, 'That I can never do, you are engraven on my heart.' On that final, heartbreaking note, George kissed his daughter goodbye and retired to his apartments. Soon afterwards, upon learning that Amelia had made no similar gift to her mother, George became so agitated that she was forced to relent. To Charlotte, Amelia gave a locket containing a lock of her own hair, but I think it's fair to say this gesture was only made to placate the distressed and ailing king.

'We have the painful duty to announce the Death of the Princess Amelia. […] She died yesterday noon, and without any pain. She was so totally exhausted by decay, as to make it almost impossible to tell when life was really extinguished. During the whole of Thursday night, and yesterday morning, her Royal Highness could scarcely be perceived to breathe, and at a quarter past twelve, at noon, this amiable object of Public solicitude departed this life.'[8]

With her goodbyes said, Princess Amelia lingered for a handful of days. She died peacefully in her bed on the afternoon of 2 November 1810, aged just 28. Her devoted sister Mary was at her side. Afterwards, Princess Mary wrote to FitzRoy to assure him that in her last moments Amelia had thought only of her lover. Amelia's dying words were, 'Tell Charles I die blessing him.'

As the court went into mourning, the princess was prepared for burial by her attendants. Dressed in her familiar nightclothes, they laid her gently in a leaden coffin that was then placed within an ornate casket of red velvet. She was interred at St George's Chapel two weeks after her death in a sombre evening ceremony, conducted by torchlight. Neither her mother nor her father were present. By then George was too unwell, and it would have gone against protocol for the queen to attend alone.

'The effect of [Princess Amelia's death] upon his MAJESTY's paternal heart, after so many severe trials during the progress of her illness, we have to deplore at this moment, though we indulge the hope that our beloved Monarch will be soon restored to his people; and that the knowledge of the termination of his Daughter's sufferings will tend to the abatement of his own.'[9]

The Morning Post speculated that the death of Princess Amelia might actually help the king recover, as he'd have one less thing to worry about. They were sorely mistaken. The loss of Amelia just a week after their last meeting was to prove too great a strain on the sickly monarch and from that day, he was rarely lucid again.

The will in which Amelia left almost everything to FitzRoy was to prove problematic for the royal family, as how were they to explain such an unexpected legatee as the king's equerry? With FitzRoy's permission it was decided that the Prince of Wales and the Duke of Cambridge, who Amelia had chosen as executors, would be officially named as the beneficiaries of the will in order to avoid any public knowledge of FitzRoy's place in the princess' heart. They assured the bereaved equerry that Amelia's wishes would be obeyed, promising that all they wanted to do was avoid any embarrassment. Sadly, the two princes were to prove far from honest and instead of following the instructions of the late princess, they began to distribute her belongings as though they were their own.

Years earlier, FitzRoy had loaned the princess the not inconsiderable sum of £5,000, most of which she had been unable to repay. Even after her death, he sought no cash settlement and asked only for the items that she had left to him in her will. Instead, Wales syphoned off the most valuable pieces and offered FitzRoy a few pieces of plate by way of a sweetener. When the furious FitzRoy complained, Wales said that Amelia had left him a snuffbox and portrait. He would graciously give these to FitzRoy if FitzRoy promised it would be an end to the matter. FitzRoy rejected the offer but grief had laid him low and though he fought on to see Amelia's wishes fulfilled, it wasn't to be. He eventually received some books and plate along with a few other assorted bits and pieces. There the matter ended.

In the years to come, FitzRoy continued his military career and was eventually promoted to the rank of general. He found a wife too, marrying Eliza Barlow in 1816, and remained in royal favour until his death in 1831. Curiously, the new Mrs FitzRoy later confirmed that she believed her husband and Amelia had been married, but no evidence exists to prove it.

The life of Princess Amelia was agonisingly short and for one who lived with such determination, at the end of her life, she simply faded away. Though the manner of her death was mercifully peaceful, Amelia went to her grave without ever having fulfilled her most dearly held ambition – to call herself the legal and rightful wife of Charles FitzRoy. She was the youngest daughter of King George III and Queen Charlotte, but she was also, conversely, the first princess to die. Her story was tragic, her life never really lived, and her loss shattered the father who had loved her with all his heart.

Little Emily never flourished, but her fighting spirit shone through. If only her health had been as strong as her determination to survive.

Afterword

'We shall see which of our […] goddesses will have the apple.'[1]

When Lady Harcourt wrote those words, it was in the sure expectation that the daughters of George III and Charlotte of Mecklenburg-Strelitz, the *goddesses*, were on course for a life in the spotlight. They were princesses, after all, accomplished, well-connected, and eminently eligible. Yet it wasn't to be. As the years passed and their father grew more unwell and their mother more resentful, the apple withered on the bough and the daughters of the House of Hanover faded into obscurity.

For the most part, these were lives that remained unfulfilled until years had passed and hopes of escape were all but abandoned. The Princess Royal alone was able to flee the cloister before the portcullis came down, trapping her sisters inside for decades. Yet these were not cyphers, nor women who were content to remain forever as daughters of the nunnery, showing slavish devotion to mother and father. They were musicians, artists, letter writers, horsewomen, philanthropists and dreamers who longed for a chance to flourish.

In these six princesses, Charlotte, Augusta, Elizabeth, Mary, Sophia, and Amelia, we see six lives lived in extraordinary circumstances. There are equerries and weddings, tragedies and the occasional quiet little triumph, and there is all too often the sense of a life cut short – sometimes literally – and a bud unable to blossom. Yet today they endure, symbols of a royal household that might have known *how* to produce offspring, but certainly wasn't sure what to do with them when they arrived. Had they been born in a different time it might all have been very different, but what ifs aren't our currency here.

Instead we bid farewell to six women, each as unique as the next, each as worthy of further investigation and each as fascinating as any of their feted or notorious brothers. Their lives are interwoven through the story of a kingdom, through monarchs and Regents and the transition from the Georgian world into the Victorian.

Four of the daughters of George III lived to see the accession of Queen Victoria and the passing of one age into another.

The era of kings was over. The era of queens had arrived.

Bibliography

Andrews, Jonathan & Scull, Andrew. *Undertaker of the Mind*. Berkeley: University of California Press, 2001.

Anonymous. *Court Life Below Stairs, Vol IV*. London: Hurst and Blackett, 1883.

Anonymous (ed.). *The Edinburgh Magazine, or Literary Miscellany, Vol VI*. Edinburgh: JS Bald, 1787.

Anonymous. *George III: His Court and Family, Vol I*. London: Henry Colburn and Co, 1820.

Anonymous. *An Historical Account of the Life and Reign of King George the Fourth*. London: G Smeeton, 1830.

Anonymous. *Leaves from the Diary of an Officer of the Guards*. London: Chapman and Hall, 1854.

Anonymous (ed.). *The London and Paris Observer; or Weekly Chronicle of Literature, Science, and the Fine Arts, Vol. IX*. Paris: A and W Galignani, 1833.

Anonymous. *Miscellanies of the Philobiblon Society, Vol XIII*. London: Whittingham and Wilkins, 1871-2.

Anonymous. *The New Jamaica Almanack, and Register, 1801*. Kingston: Stevenson and Aikman, 1801.

Anonymous. *The Parliamentary History of England from the Earliest Period to the Year 1803, XVII*. London: Longman, Hurst, Rees, Orme, & Brown, 1813.

Anonymous. *Reports on the Manuscripts of JB Fortescue, Esq*. London: Royal Commission on Historical Manuscripts, 1899.

Anson, Sir Archibald Edward Harbord. *About Others and Myself, 1745-1920*. London: John Murray, 1920.

Aspinall, Arthur (ed.). *The Correspondence of George, Prince of Wales: Vol I*. London: Cassell, 1963.

Aspinall, Arthur (ed.). *The Correspondence of George, Prince of Wales: Vol II*. London: Cassell, 1963.

Aspinall, Arthur (ed.). *The Correspondence of George, Prince of Wales: Vol II*. Oxford: Oxford University Press, 1971.

Aspinall, Arthur. *The Correspondence of George, Prince of Wales, Volume VI*. Oxford: Oxford University Press, 1971.

Aspinall Arthur (ed.). *Later Correspondence of George III: December 1783 to January 1793*. Cambridge: Cambridge University Press, 1920.

Aspinall, Arthur. *The Later Correspondence of George III, Vol II*. Cambridge: Cambridge University Press, 1962.

Aspinall, Arthur. *The Later Correspondence of George III, Vol III*. Cambridge: Cambridge University Press, 1967.

Aspinall, Arthur. *The Later Correspondence of George III, Vol IV*. Cambridge: Cambridge University Press, 1968.

Aspinall, Arthur. *The Later Correspondence of George III, Vol V*. Cambridge: Cambridge University Press, 1970.

Aspinall, Arthur (ed.). *Letters of the Princess Charlotte, 1811-1817*. London: Home and Van Thal, 1949.

Baker, Kenneth. *George III: A Life in Caricature*. London: Thames & Hudson, 2007.

Baker, Kenneth. *George IV: A Life in Caricature*. London: Thames & Hudson, 2005.

Baudino, Isabelle & Carré, Jacques. *The Invisible Woman*. London: Routledge, 2017.

Beatty, Michael A. *The English Royal Family of America, from Jamestown to the American Revolution*. Jefferson: McFarland & Company, Inc, 2003.

Belsham, William. *Memoirs of the Kings of Great Britain of the House of Brunswic-Luneburg, Vol I*. London: C Dilly, 1793.

Belsham, William. *Memoirs of the Reign of George III to the Session of Parliament Ending AD 1793, Vol III*. London: GG and J Robinson, 1801.

Black, Jeremy. *George III: America's Last King*. New Haven: Yale University Press, 2008.

Black, Jeremy. *The Hanoverians: The History of a Dynasty*. London: Hambledon and London, 2007.

Buckingham and Chandos, Duke of. *Memoirs of the Court of George IV, Vol I*. London: Hurst and Blackett, 1859.

Burney, Frances. *The Diary and Letters of Frances Burney, Madame D'Arblay, Vol I*. Boston: Little, Brown and Company, 1910.

Burney, Frances. *The Diary and Letters of Frances Burney, Madame D'Arblay, Vol II*. Boston: Little, Brown and Company, 1910.

Burney, Frances. *Diary and Letters of Madame D'Arblay, Vol VI*. London: Henry Colburn, 1854.

Bury, Lady Charlotte Campbell. *Diary Illustrative of the Times of George the Fourth: Vol II*. London: Carey, Lea and Blanchard, 1838.

Bury, Lady Charlotte Campbell. *Diary Illustrative of the Times of George the Fourth: Vol III*. London: Henry Colburn, 1839.

Campbell Orr, Clarissa. *Queenship in Europe 1660–1815: The Role of the Consort*. Cambridge: Cambridge University Press, 2004.

Catania, Steven, 'Brandy Nan and Farmer George: Public Perceptions of Royal Health and the Demystification of English Monarchy During the Long Eighteenth Century' (2014). *Dissertations*. Paper 1255. http://ecommons.luc.edu/luc_diss/1255

Chambers, Robert. *The Book of Days, Vol II*. London: W&R Chambers, 1864.

Chapman, Hester W. *Caroline Matilda, Queen of Denmark, 1751–75*. London: Cape, 1971.

Chapman, Hester W. *Privileged Persons*. London: Reynal & Hitchcock, 1966.

Childe-Pemberton, William. *The Romance of Princess Amelia*. London: G Bell & Sons, 1910.

Clarke. *The Georgian Era: Volume I*. London, Vizetelly, Branston and Co., 1832.

Coke, Lady Mary. *The Letters of Lady Mary Coke: 1756-1767*. Bath: Kingsmead, 1970.

Cole, Hubert. *Beau Brummell*. London: HarperCollins Distribution Services, 1977.

Craig, William Marshall. *Memoir of Her Majesty Sophia Charlotte of Mecklenburg Strelitz, Queen of Great Britain*. Liverpool: Henry Fisher, 1818.

Craik, George Lillie & MacFarlane, Charles (ed.). *The Pictorial History of England During the Reign of King George the Third: Vol I*. London: Charles Knight and Co, 1841.

Curzon, Catherine. *Kings of Georgian Britain*. Barnsley: Pen & Sword, 2017.

Curzon, Catherine. *Queens of Georgian Britain*. Barnsley: Pen & Sword, 2017.

Curzon, Catherine. *The Scandal of George III's Court*. Barnsley: Pen & Sword, 2018.

Delves Broughton, Vernon (ed.). *Court and Private Life in the Time of Queen Charlotte*. London: Richard Bentley, 1887.

Dickenson, Mary Hamilton. *Mary Hamilton: Afterwards Mrs. John Dickenson, at Court and at Home*. London: John Murray, 1925.

Donne, Bodham W (ed.). *The Correspondence of King George the Third with Lord North from 1768 to 1783: Vol I*. London: John Murray, 1867.

Doran, John. *Lives of the Queens of England of the House of Hanover, Volume I*. New York: Redfield, 1855.

Doran, John. *Lives of the Queens of England of the House of Hanover, Volume II*. Boston, Francis A Niccolls & Co, 1900.

Fitzgerald, Percy. *The Good Queen Charlotte*. London: Downey & Co, 1899.

Fitzgerald, Percy. *The Royal Dukes and Princesses of the Family of George III, Vol I*. London: Tinsley Brothers, 1882.

Fitzgerald, Percy. *The Royal Dukes and Princesses of the Family of George III, Vol II*. London: Tinsley Brothers, 1882.

Fraser, Flora. *Princesses: The Six Daughters of George III*. Edinburgh: A&C Black, 2012.

Gillett, Eric Walkey (ed.). *Elizabeth Ham, by Herself*. London: Faber & Faber Ltd, 1945.

Glenbervie, Sylvester Douglas. *The Diaries of Sylvester Douglas, Lord Glenbervie*. London: Constable & Co Ltd, 1928.

Hadlow, Janice. *The Strangest Family: The Private Lives of George III, Queen Charlotte and the Hanoverians*. London: William Collins, 2014.

Haggard, John. *Reports of Cases Argued and Determined in the Ecclesiastical Courts at Doctor's Commons, and in the High Court of Delegates, Vol I*. London: W Benning, 1829.

Hague, William. *William Pitt the Younger*. London: Harper Perennial, 2005.

Hall, Matthew. *The Royal Princesses of England*. London: George Routledge and Sons, 1871.

Harcourt, Leveson Vernon (ed.). *The Diaries and Correspondence of the Right Hon. George Rose, Vol II*. London: Richard Bentley, 1860.

Hayward, A (ed.). *Diaries of a Lady of Quality from 1797 to 1844*. London: Longman, Green, Longman, Egberts & Green, 1864.

Heard, Kate. *High Spirits: The Comic Art of Thomas Rowlandson*. London: Royal Collection Trust, 2013.

Hedley, Owen. *Queen Charlotte*. London: J Murray, 1975.

Bibliography

Hibbert, Christopher. *George III: A Personal History*. London: Viking, 1998.

Hibbert, Christopher. *George IV*. London: Penguin, 1998.

Hill, Constance. *Fanny Burney at the Court of Queen Charlotte*. London: John Lane, 1912.

Holt, Edward. *The Public and Domestic Life of His Late Most Gracious Majesty, George the Third, Vol I*. London: Sherwood, Neely and Jones, 1820.

Holt, Edward. *The Public and Domestic Life of His Late Most Gracious Majesty, George the Third, Vol II*. London: Sherwood, Neely and Jones, 1820.

Home, James A. *Letters of Lady Louisa Stuart to Miss Louisa Clinton*. Edinburgh: D Douglas, 1901.

Horrins, Johan. *Memoirs of a Trait in the Character of George III of These United Kingdoms*. London: W Edwards, 1835.

Howard, John Jackson and Crisp, Frederick Arthur (eds.). *Visitation of England and Wales, Volume 5*. Privately published, 1897.

Huish, Robert. *The History of the Life and Reign of William the Fourth*. London: William Emans, 1837.

Huish, Robert. *Memoirs of George the Fourth, Vol I*. London: T Kelly, 1830.

Huish, Robert. *Memoirs of Her Late Majesty Caroline, Queen of Great Britain*. London: T Kelly, 1821.

Hunt, Margaret. *Women in Eighteenth-Century Europe*. New York: Routledge, 2010.

Ilchester, Countess of & Stavordale, Lord (eds.). *The Life and Letters of Lady Sarah Lennox*. London: John Murray, 1902.

Iremonger, Lucille. *Love and the Princesses*. New York: Thomas Y Crowell Company, 1958.

Jesse Heneage, J. *Memoirs of the Life and Reign of King George the Third, Vol II*. London: Tinsley Brothers, 1867.

Jesse Heneage, J. *Memoirs of the Life and Reign of King George the Third, Vol III*. London: Richard Bentley, 1843.

Jesse Heneage, J. *Memoirs of the Life and Reign of King George the Third, Vol IV*. Boston, LC Page & Company, 1902.

Kiste, John van der. *George III's Children*. Stroud: The History Press, 2004.

Kiste, John van der. *The Georgian Princesses*. Stroud: The History Press, 2013.

Knight, Cornelia. *Autobiography of Miss Cornelia Knight, Vol I*. London: WH Allen, 1861.

Knight, Cornelia. *Autobiography of Miss Cornelia Knight, Vol II*. Cambridge: Cambridge University Press, 1861.

Lancelott, Francis. *The Queens of England and Their Times: Volume II*. New York: D Appleton and Co, 1859.

Lehman, H Eugene. *Lives of England's Reigning and Consort Queens*. Bloomington: AuthorHouse, 2011.

Llanover, Lady. *The Autobiography and Correspondence of Mary Granville, Mrs Delaney, Vol II*. London, Richard Bentley, 1862.

Llanover, Lady. *The Autobiography and Correspondence of Mary Granville, Mrs Delaney, Vol III*. London, Richard Bentley, 1862.

Lloyd, Hannibal Evans. *George IV: Memoirs of His Life and Reign, Interspersed with Numerous Personal Anecdotes*. London: Treuttel and Würtz, 1830.

Longford, Elizabeth. *The Oxford Book of Royal Anecdotes*. Oxford: Oxford University Press, 1989.

Melville, Lewis. *Farmer George, Vol I*. London: Sir Isaac Pitman and Sons, Ltd, 1907.

Minto, Emma Eleanor Elizabeth (ed.). *Life and Letters of Sir Gilbert Elliot First Earl of Minto from 1751 to 1806*. London: Longmans, 1874.

Montgomery-Campbell, M (ed.). *Records of Stirring Times*. London: William Heinemann, 1908.

Müller, F Max (ed.). *Memoirs of Baron Stockmar, Vol I*. London: Longmans, Green, and Co, 1873.

O'Meara, Barry E. *Napoleon in Exile, Vol II*. New York: Redfield, 1853.

Oulton, CW. *Authentic and Impartial Memoirs of Her Late Majesty: Charlotte Queen of Great Britain and Ireland*. London: J Robins and Co, 1818.

Papendiek, Charlotte. *Court and Private Life in the Time of Queen Charlotte, Vol I*. London: Richard Bentley & Son, 1887.

Papendiek, Charlotte. *Court and Private Life in the Time of Queen Charlotte, Vol II*. London: Richard Bentley & Son, 1887.

Percy, Sholto and Percy, Reuben. *The Percy Anecdotes: Volume IV*. London: T Boys, 1823.

Peters, TJ & Beveridge, A, "The Blindness, Deafness and Madness of King George III: Psychiatric Interactions" (2010). *The Journal of the*

Royal College of Physicians of Edinburgh, Vol 40: Issue 1. https://www.rcpe.ac.uk/sites/default/files/peters_1.pdf

Plowden, Alison. *Caroline and Charlotte*. Stroud: The History Press, 2011.

Reece, Richard. *The Medical Guide*. London: Longman, Hurst, Rees, Orme, and Brown, 1813.

Reid, Hamilton, W. *Memoirs of the Public and Private Life of Napoleon Bonaparte*. London: Sherwood, Gilbert, and Piper, 1826.

Roberts, Jane. *Royal Landscape: The Gardens and Parks of Windsor*. New Haven: Yale University Press, 1910.

Roelker Curtis, Edith. *Lady Sarah Lennox: An Irrepressible Stuart*. New York: G P Putnam's Sons, 1946.

Sanders, Margaret. *Intimate Letters of England's Queens*. Stroud: Amberley, 2014.

Sinclair-Stevenson, Christopher. *Blood Royal: The Illustrious House of Hanover*. London: Faber & Faber, 2012.

Smith, EA. *George IV*. New Haven: Yale University Press, 1999.

Smith, William James (ed.). *The Greville Papers: Vol III*. London: John Murray, 1853.

Spencer, Sarah. *Correspondence of Sarah Spencer Lady Lyttelton 1787–1870*. London: John Murray, 1912.

Stuart, Dorothy Margaret. *The Daughters of George III*. London: Fonthill Media, 1939.

Taylor, Ernest (ed.). *The Taylor Papers*. London: Longmans, Green, and Co, 1913.

Thackeray, William Makepeace. *The Works of William Makepeace Thackeray: Vol XIX*. London: Smith, Elder, & Co, 1869.

Tillyard, Stella. *A Royal Affair: George III and his Troublesome Siblings*. London: Vintage, 2007.

Tinniswood, Adrian. *Behind the Throne*. London: Random House, 2018.

Toynbee, Paget. *The Letters of Horace Walpole, Vol IX*. Oxford: The Clarendon Press, 1903.

Toynbee, Paget. *The Letters of Horace Walpole, Vol XI*. Oxford: The Clarendon Press, 1903.

Toynbee, Paget. *The Letters of Horace Walpole, Vol XIII*. Oxford: The Clarendon Press, 1903.

Toynbee, Paget. *The Letters of Horace Walpole, Vol XIV*. Oxford: The Clarendon Press, 1903.

Toynbee, Paget. *The Letters of Horace Walpole, Vol XV.* Oxford: The Clarendon Press, 1903.

Toynbee, Paget. *Supplement to the Letters of Horace Walpole, Vol III.* Oxford: The Clarendon Press, 1903.

Toynbee, Paget. *Supplement to the Letters of Horace Walpole, Vol VII.* Oxford: The Clarendon Press, 1903.

Urban, Sylvanus. *The Gentleman's Magazine, Volume XII.* London: William Pickering; John Bowyer Nichols and Son, 1840.

Urban, Sylvanus. *The Gentleman's Magazine, Volume XIV.* London: William Pickering; John Bowyer Nichols and Son, 1840.

Urban, Sylvanus. *The Gentleman's Magazine, Volume XCVIII.* London: JB Nichols and Son, 1828.

Walpole, Horace. *The Last Journals of Horace Walpole During the Reign of George III from 1771–1783.* London: John Lane, 1910.

Walpole, Horace. *Letters of Horace Walpole, Earl of Orford to Sir Horace Mann.* London: Richard Bentley, 1833.

Walpole, Horace. *Letters of Horace Walpole, Earl of Orford, to Sir Horace Mann, Vol I.* London: Richard Bentley, 1843.

Walpole, Horace. *Letters of Horace Walpole, Earl of Orford to Sir Horace Mann, Vol II.* Philadelphia: Lea & Blanchard, 1844.

Walpole, Horace. *Letters of Horace Walpole, Earl of Orford to Sir Horace Mann, Vol III.* London: Richard Bentley, 1833.

Walpole, Horace. *Letters of Horace Walpole, Earl of Orford to Sir Horace Mann, Vol IV.* London: Richard Bentley, 1844.

Walpole, Horace. *The Letters of Horace Walpole: Vol I.* London: Lea and Blanchard, 1842.

Walpole, Horace. *The Letters of Horace Walpole: Vol II.* New York: Dearborn, 1832.

Walpole, Horace. *Memoirs of the Reign of King George the Third: Vol I.* Philadelphia: Lea & Blanchard, 1845.

Walpole, Horace. *Memoirs of the Reign of King George the Third: Vol II.* Philadelphia: Lea & Blanchard, 1845.

Walpole, Horace. *Memoirs of the Reign of King George the Third: Vol III.* London: Richard Bentley, 1845.

Walpole, Horace. *Memoirs of the Reign of King George the Third: Vol IV.* London: Richard Bentley, 1845.

Walpole, Horace and Doran, John (ed.). *Journal of the Reign of King George the Third, Vol I.* London, Richard Bentley, 1859.

Walpole, Horace and Doran, John (ed.). *Journal of the Reign of King George the Third, Vol II*. London, Richard Bentley, 1859.

Watkins, John. *The Life and Times of William the Fourth*. London: Fisher, Son, and Jackson, 1831.

Watkins, John. *Memoirs of Her Most Excellent Majesty Sophia-Charlotte, Queen of Great Britain*. London: Richard Bentley, 1845.

Watson, Samuel. *The Gentleman's and Citizen's Almanack*. S Powell: Dublin, 1772.

Weigall, Rose. *A Brief Memoir of the Princess Charlotte of Wales*. London: John Murray, 1874.

Williams, Thomas. *Memoirs of Her Late Majesty Queen Charlotte*. London: W Simpkin and R Marshall, 1819.

Williams, Thomas. *Memoirs of His Late Majesty George III*. London: W Simpkin and R Marshall, 1820.

Woolsey, Sarah Chauncey. *The Diary and Letters of Frances Burney, Madame D'Arblay, Vol I*. Boston: Little, Brown, and Company, 1910.

Woolsey, Sarah Chauncey. *The Diary and Letters of Frances Burney, Madame D'Arblay, Vol II*. Boston: Little, Brown, and Company, 1910.

Yorke, Philip (ed). *Letters of Princess Elizabeth of England*. London: T Fisher Unwin, 1898.

Newspapers

All newspaper clippings are reproduced © The British Library Board; in addition to those cited, innumerable newspapers were consulted.

Caledonian Mercury (Edinburgh, Scotland), Thursday, 24 September, 1840; Issue 18832.

Daily News (London, England), Friday, 1 May, 1857; Issue 3419.

General Evening Post (London, England), 15 February, 1772 - 18 February, 1772; Issue 5984.

General Evening Post (London, England), 11 March, 1790 - 13 March, 1790; Issue 8799.

General Evening Post (London, England), 18 May, 1797 - 20 May, 1797; Issue 10074.

Hampshire Telegraph and Sussex Chronicle etc (Portsmouth, England), Monday, 5 November, 1810; Issue 578.

Jackson's Oxford Journal (Oxford, England), Saturday, 10 January, 1829; Issue 3950.

London Chronicle (London, England), 7 August, 1783 - 9 August, 1783; Issue 4177.

London Chronicle (London, England), 30 August, 1787 - 1 September, 1787; Issue 4809.

London Evening Post (London, England), 8 September, 1761 - 10 September, 1761; Issue 5283.

London Evening Post (London, England), 30 September, 1766 - 2 October, 1766; Issue 6073.

London Gazette (London, England), 4 November, 1777 - 8 November, 1777; Issue 11820.

London Packet or New Evening Post (London, England), 8 April, 1772 - 10 April, 1772; Issue 384.

London Packet or New Lloyd's Evening Post (London, England), 15 April, 1772 - 17 April, 1772; Issue 387.

The Morning Chronicle (London, England), Saturday, 2 February, 1811; Issue 13022.

The Morning Chronicle (London, England), Saturday, 19 February, 1814; Issue 13976.

The Morning Chronicle (London, England), Tuesday, 23 July, 1816; Issue 14734.

The Morning Chronicle (London, England), Thursday, 16 March, 1820; Issue 15875.

The Morning Chronicle (London, England), Monday, 29 May, 1848; Issue 24524.

Morning Chronicle and London Advertiser (London, England), Friday, 26 April, 1776; Issue 2163.

Morning Chronicle and London Advertiser (London, England), Tuesday, 3 June, 1788; Issue 5949.

Morning Herald (London, England), Thursday, 1 January, 1789; Issue 2558.

Morning Herald (London, England), Monday, 9 March, 1789; Issue 2615.

The Morning Post (London, England), Monday, 5 November, 1810; Issue 12406.

The Morning Post (London, England), Thursday, 17 November, 1814; Issue 13675.

The Morning Post (London, England), Monday, 3 June, 1816; Issue 14156.

The Morning Post (London, England), Tuesday, 16 July, 1816; Issue 14193.

Morning Post (London, England), Thursday, 5 February, 1818; Issue 14679.

Morning Post (London, England), Wednesday, 8 April, 1818; Issue 14732.

The Morning Post (London, England), Tuesday, 17 March, 1829; Issue 18177.

The Morning Post (London, England), Tuesday, 2 December, 1834; Issue 19964.

Morning Post (London, England), Wednesday, 19 November, 1851; Issue 24318.

Morning Post and Daily Advertiser (London, England), Tuesday, 6 June, 1786; Issue 4150.

Morning Post and Daily Advertiser (London, England), Friday, 20 March, 1789; Issue 4985.

Public Advertiser (London, England), Tuesday, 30 September, 1766; Issue 9958.

Public Advertiser (London, England), Wednesday, 7 May, 1783; Issue 15271.

Public Advertiser (London, England), Monday, 9 June, 1788; Issue 16814.

St. James's Chronicle or the British Evening Post (London, England), 8 November, 1768 - 10 November, 1768; Issue 1201.

The Standard (London, England), Thursday, 16 January, 1840; Issue 4860.

The Standard (London, England), Wednesday, 23 September, 1840; Issue 5074.

Sun (London, England), Wednesday, 2 October, 1799; Issue 2193.

True Briton (1793) (London, England), Monday, 17 April, 1797; Issue 1345.

Westminster Journal and London Political Miscellany (London, England), Saturday, 26 May, 1770; Issue 1316.

Whitehall Evening Post (1770) (London, England), 21 December, 1797 - 23 December, 1797; Issue 7974.

Whitehall Evening Post or London Intelligencer (London, England), 26 October, 1769 - 28 October, 1769; Issue 3677.

Websites Consulted

British History Online (http://www.british-history.ac.uk)

British Newspapers 1600–1950 (http://gdc.gale.com/products/19thcenturybritish-library-newspapers-part-i-and-part-ii/)

Georgian Papers Online, Royal Archives, Windsor (https://gpp.
royalcollection.org.uk)

Hansard (http://hansard.millbanksystems.com/index.html)

Historical Texts (http://historicaltexts.jisc.ac.uk)

House of Commons Parliamentary Papers (http://parlipapers.chadwyck.
co.uk/marketing/index.jsp)

JSTOR (www.jstor.org)

The National Archives (http://www.nationalarchives.gov.uk)

Oxford Dictionary of National Biography (http://www.oxforddnb.com)

Queen Victoria's Journals (http://www.queenvictoriasjournals.org)

State Papers Online (https://www.gale.com/intl/primary-sources/
statepapers-online)

The Times Digital Archive (http://gale.cengage.co.uk/times-
digitalarchive/times-digital-archive-17852006.aspx)

Endnotes

Introduction

1. Longford, Elizabeth (1989). *The Oxford Book of Royal Anecdotes*. Oxford: Oxford University Press, p.327.

A King, A Queen, and a Family of Fifteen

1. *London Evening Post* (London, England), 8 September 1761 – 10 September 1761; Issue 5283.
2. George became king on 25 October 1760, on the death of King George II.
3. Roelker Curtis, Edith (1946). *Lady Sarah Lennox: An Irrepressible Stuart*. New York: G P Putnam's Sons, p.107.
4. Walpole, Horace (1843). *Letters of Horace Walpole, Earl of Orford, to Sir Horace Mann, Vol I*. London: Richard Bentley, p.41.
5. Roelker Curtis, Edith (1946). *Lady Sarah Lennox: An Irrepressible Stuart*. New York: G P Putnam's Sons, p.93.
6. *London Evening Post* (London, England), 30 September, 1766 – 2 October 1766; Issue 6073.
7. Coke, Lady Mary (1970). *The Letters of Lady Mary Coke: 1756-1767*. Bath: Kingsmead, p.54.
8. The marriage between Caroline Matilda and Christian VII was a famous disaster. As the king sank into madness, his queen and his physician, Johann Friedrich Struensee, became lovers and eventually took control of the kingdom. The fallout was brutal, violent and shattering for all involved. Lovers of scandal can discover the full story of what happened when Caroline Matilda went to Denmark in my book, *The Scandals of George III's Court* (Pen & Sword, 2018).
9. For royal-watchers with a penchant for lists, the seven holders of the title so far have been Mary (1631-1660), daughter of Charles I, Anne (1709-1759), daughter of George II, our own Charlotte, Victoria (1840-1901), daughter of Victoria, Louise (1867-1931), daughter of Edward VII, Mary (1897-1965), daughter of George V, and the current incumbent, Anne (1950-present), the daughter of Elizabeth II.
10. *Public Advertiser* (London, England), Tuesday, 30 September 1766; Issue 9958.

11. Charlotte's father, Duke Charles Louis Frederick of Mecklenburg, had died many years earlier in 1752. Her mother, Elisabeth Albertine of Saxe-Hildburghausen, passed away in 1761 as Charlotte prepared to travel to England to marry George III.

12. *St. James's Chronicle or the British Evening Post* (London, England), 8 November 1768 – 10 November 1768; Issue 1201.

13. Hedley, Olwen (1975). *Queen Charlotte*. London: John Murray, p.104.

14. *Whitehall Evening Post or London Intelligencer* (London, England), 26. October 1769 – 28 October 1769; Issue 3677.

15. *Westminster Journal and London Political Miscellany* (London, England), Saturday, 26 May 1770; Issue 1316.

16. Woolsey, Sarah Chauncey (1910). *The Diary and Letters of Frances Burney, Madame D'Arblay, Vol I*. Boston: Little, Brown, and Company, p.366.

17. *Morning Post and Daily Advertiser* (London, England), Tuesday, 6 June 1786; Issue 4150.

18. Smith, William James (ed.) (1853). *The Greville Papers: Vol III*. London: John Murray, p.115.

19. Ibid.

20. Georgian Papers Online (http://gpp.rct.uk, March 2019) GEO/ADD/15/8156 Letter from Queen Charlotte to Lady Charlotte Finch, 17 April 1775.

21. Maria's parents were Edward "Neddy" Walpole, son of Sir Robert Walpole, and Dorothy Clement, a beautiful but poor young lady who had been employed on a dust cart in London. Though their loving relationship lasted until Dorothy's early death in 1739 and produced four children, the couple never married.

22. For the full story of sex, murder and scandal, see my own book, *The Imprisoned Princess: The Scandalous Life of Sophia Dorothea of Celle* (Pen & Sword Books, 2020).

23. Anonymous (1833) (ed.). *The London and Paris Observer; or Weekly Chronicle of Literature, Science, and the Fine Arts, Vol. IX*. Paris: A and W Galignani, p.234.

24. Sixteen quarterings is, to some, the holy grail of hereditary lineage. It suggests that the preceding four generations of ancestry has been composed exclusively of nobility.

25. Craik, George Lillie & MacFarlane, Charles (1841) (ed.). *The Pictorial History of England During the Reign of King George the Third: Vol I*. London: Charles Knight and Co, p.126.

26. Frederick North, 2nd Earl of Guilford, was Prime Minister from 1770 to 1782. His term was not the most settled!

27. Donne, W Bodham (1867) (ed.). *The Correspondence of King George the Third with Lord North from 1768 to 1783, Vol I*. London: John Murray, p.91.

28. Although the Prince of Wales' marriage to Maria Fitzherbert remained a secret from his father, not all of George's sons were so fortunate. When Prince Augustus Frederick, Duke of Sussex, married Lady Augusta Murray without his father's consent in 1793, the furious king had the marriage annulled the

following year. Despite this, the couple stayed together with their two children until 1801, when they finally split for good.

29. *General Evening Post* (London, England), 15 February 1772 – 18 February 1772; Issue 5984.

30. The 19-year-old Princess Louisa died in 1768, a victim of tuberculosis.

31. Princess Louise Auguste was a great favourite at court. *La petite Struensee*, as some called her, eventually became the mistress of her own marital court as Duchess of Schleswig-Holstein-Sonderburg-Augustenburg.

32. For the whole gory and saucy story, see my own book, *The Scandals of George III's Court* (Pen & Sword, 2018).

33. *London Packet or New Lloyd's Evening Post* (London, England), 15 April 1772 – 17 April 1772; Issue 387.

34. Walpole, Horace (1910). *The Last Journals of Horace Walpole During the Reign of George III from 1771–1783*. London: John Lane, p.125.

35. William Finch was a parliamentarian and diplomat. He and Lady Charlotte were separated after an incident in which he beat her and threw her downstairs.

36. Georgian Papers Online (http://gpp.rct.uk, March 2019) GEO/ADD/15/8154 Letter from Queen Charlotte to Lady Charlotte Finch, 1774-1775.

37. Ibid.

38. Georgian Papers Online (http://gpp.rct.uk, March 2019) GEO/ADD/15/8155 Letter from Lady Charlotte Finch to Queen Charlotte, 31 October 1774.

39. Ibid.

40. *Morning Chronicle and London Advertiser* (London, England), Friday, 26 April 1776; Issue 2163.

41. Frederick and Mary were married in 1740 and together had four children, three of whom survived infancy. Their marriage was an unhappy one and Frederick was a violent spouse. Eventually the couple formally separated in 1755 and Mary remained on the continent and made her home in Denmark, where she raised her surviving children.

42. *London Gazette* (London, England), 4 November 1777 – 8 November 1777; Issue 11820.

43. Oulton, Walley Chamberlain (1819). *Authentic and Impartial Memoirs of Her Late Majesty, Charlotte, Queen of Great Britain and Ireland*. London: J Robins and Co, p.175.

44. Papendiek, Charlotte Louise Henrietta (1887). *Court and Private Life in the Time of Queen Charlotte, Vol I*. London: T Bentley & Son, pp.41-42.

45. Later to reign as King William IV.

46. Georgian Papers Online (http://gpp.rct.uk, March 2019) GEO/ADD/4/17 Letter from Queen Charlotte to Prince William, 4 September 1782.

47. *Public Advertiser* (London, England), Wednesday, 7 May 7 1783; Issue 15271.

48. Walpole, Horace (1844). *Letters of Horace Walpole, Earl of Orford to Sir Horace Mann, Vol II*. Philadelphia: Lea & Blanchard, p.298.

49. Georgian Papers Online (http://gpp.rct.uk, March 2019) GEO/ADD/4/17 Letter from Queen Charlotte to Prince William, 4 September 1782.

50. Queen Charlotte's physician, William Hunter, died on 30 March 1783. Princess Amelia was delivered by James Ford, who later became the queen's physician in 1788.

51. *London Chronicle* (London, England), 7 August 1783 – 9 August 1783; Issue 4177.

52. Papendiek, Charlotte Louise Henrietta (1887). *Court and Private Life in the Time of Queen Charlotte, Vol I*. London: T Bentley & Son, p.197.

Charlotte, Princess Royal (29 September 1766 – 5 October 1828)

1. Watkins, John (1819). *Memoirs of Her Most Excellent Majesty Sophia-Charlotte, Queen of Great Britain*. London: Henry Colburn, p.353.

2. Anson, Sir Archibald Edward Harbord (1920). *About Others and Myself, 1745-1920*. London: John Murray, p.17.

3. Aspinall A (ed.) (1920). *Later Correspondence of George III: December 1783 to January 1793*. Cambridge: Cambridge University Press, p.14.

4. The prince renounced his position as heir in favour of his brother. Despite the challenges he faced he did eventually marry, taking as his bride Princess Louise of Orange-Nassau. Though their marriage was childless and she was more of a carer than a wife to her husband, the couple were happy together and their union was a loving one.

5. Cole, Hubert (1977). *Beau Brummell*. London: HarperCollins Distribution Services, p.26.

6. Percy, Sholto and Percy, Reuben (1823). *The Percy Anecdotes: Volume IV*. London: T Boys, p.126.

7. *London Chronicle* (London, England), 30 August 1787 – 1 September 1787; Issue 4809.

8. Woolsey, Sarah Chauncey (1910). *The Diary and Letters of Frances Burney, Madame D'Arblay, Vol I*. Boston: Little, Brown, and Company, p.149.

9. The couple married in secret in 1785. The marriage was illegitimate under the terms of the Royal Marriages Act 1772, which required the heir to the throne to secure approval from the reigning monarch before any marriage could go ahead. The act was intended to ensure that the throne would not fall into inappropriate – or Catholic - hands. Though marrying in contravention of the act didn't mean that the party concerned would be removed from the line of succession, it did mean that the marriage wasn't recognised, rendering any children born of such a union illegitimate and exempt from succeeding to the throne.

10. Watkins, John (1819). *Memoirs of Her Most Excellent Majesty Sophia-Charlotte, Queen of Great Britain*. London: Henry Colburn, p.378.

11. Ibid., p.392.

12. Their daughter, Catherine, would eventually become Queen of Westphalia as the bride of Jérôme Bonaparte.

13. Aspinall, Arthur (1962). *The Later Correspondence of George III, Vol II*. Cambridge: Cambridge University Press, p.31.

14. Ibid.

15. Anonymous. *Reports on the Manuscripts of JB Fortescue, Esq* (1899). London: Royal Commission on Historical Manuscripts, p.147.

16. *True Briton* (1793) (London, England), Monday, 17 April 1797; Issue 1345.

17. Woolsey, Sarah Chauncey (1910). *The Diary and Letters of Frances Burney, Madame D'Arblay, Vol II*. Boston: Little, Brown, and Company, p.366.

18. *General Evening Post* (London, England), 18 May 1797 - 20 May 1797; Issue 10074.

19. *Whitehall Evening Post* (1770) (London, England) 21 December 1797 – 23 December 1797; Issue 7974.

20. Aspinall, Arthur (1967). *The Later Correspondence of George III, Vol III*. Cambridge: Cambridge University Press, p.58.

21 Ibid.

22. Ibid., p.446.

23. Ibid., p.606.

24. Reid, Hamilton, W (1826). *Memoirs of the Public and Private Life of Napoleon Bonaparte*. London: Sherwood, Gilbert, and Piper, p.349.

25. *The Morning Chronicle* (London, England), Saturday, 19 February 1814; Issue 13976.

26. Home, James A (1901). *Letters of Lady Louisa Stuart to Miss Louisa Clinton*. Edinburgh: D Douglas, p.75.

27. Ibid.

28. Urban, Sylvanus (1828). *The Gentleman's Magazine, Volume XCVIII*. London: JB Nichols and Son, p.567.

Princess Augusta Sophia of the United Kingdom
(8 November 1768 – 22 September 1840)

1. Georgian Papers Online (http://gpp.rct.uk, March 2019) GEO/ADD/10/1 Letter from Princess Augusta to Queen Charlotte, 26 December 1777.

2. Burney, Frances (1910). *The Diary and Letters of Frances Burney, Madame D'Arblay, Vol II*. Boston: Little, Brown and Company, p.27.

3. Papendiek, Charlotte Louise Henrietta (1887). *Court and Private Life in the Time of Queen Charlotte, Vol II*. London: T Bentley & Son, p.208.

4. Woolsey, Sarah Chauncey (1910). *The Diary and Letters of Frances Burney, Madame D'Arblay, Vol II*. Boston: Little, Brown, and Company, p.146.

5. Anonymous (1854). *Leaves from the Diary of an Officer of the Guards*. London: Chapman and Hall, p.80.

6. Georgian Papers Online (http://gpp.rct.uk, March 2019) GEO/ADD/10/12 Letter from Princess Augusta to George, Prince of Wales, 12 August 1797.

7. Aspinall, Arthur (ed.) (1971). *The Correspondence of George, Prince of Wales: Vol II*. Oxford: Oxford University Press, p.367.

8. *The Morning Chronicle* (London, England), Saturday, 2 February 1811; Issue 13022.

9. Urban, Sylvanus (1840). *The Gentleman's Magazine, Volume XIV.* London: William Pickering; John Bowyer Nichols and Son, p.537.

10. Georgian Papers Online (http://gpp.rct.uk, March 2019) GEO/ADD/10/52 Letter from Queen Charlotte to Princesses Augusta, Elizabeth, Mary and Sophia, 2 April 1812.

11. Ibid.

12. Georgian Papers Online (http://gpp.rct.uk, March 2019) GEO/ADD/10/59 Letter from Princess Augusta to the Prince Regent, 23 January 1812.

13. Georgian Papers Online (http://gpp.rct.uk, March 2019) GEO/ADD/10/56 Letter from Princess Augusta to the Prince Regent, 5 March 1812.

14. Ibid.

15. Ibid.

16. Fitzgerald, Percy (1882). *The Royal Dukes and Princesses of the Family of George III, Vol II*. London: Tinsley Brothers, p.18.

17. *The Morning Post* (London, England), Thursday, 17 November 1814; Issue 13675.

18. Fitzgerald, Percy (1882). *The Royal Dukes and Princesses of the Family of George III, Vol I*. London: Tinsley Brothers, p.265.

19. Ibid.

20. Fitzgerald, Percy (1882). *The Royal Dukes and Princesses of the Family of George III, Vol II*. London: Tinsley Brothers, p.320.

21. Chambers, Robert (1864). *The Book of Days, Vol II*. London: W&R Chambers, p.369.

22. *Jackson's Oxford Journal* (Oxford, England), Saturday, 10 January 1829; Issue 3950.

23. *Caledonian Mercury* (Edinburgh, Scotland), Thursday, 24 September 1840; Issue 18832.

24. *The Standard* (London, England), Wednesday, 23 September 1840; Issue 5074.

25. Urban, Sylvanus (1840). *The Gentleman's Magazine, Volume XIV.* London: William Pickering; John Bowyer Nichols and Son, p.537.

Princess Elizabeth of the United Kingdom
(22 May 1770 – 10 January 1840)

1. Mary Delany was particularly noted for her skills as a paper-cutter, in which she used brightly coloured paper to create vivid works of art. She created almost

a thousand highly accurate botanical illustrations in this way and George and Charlotte were enthusiastic patrons of her work.

2. Papendiek, Charlotte Louise Henrietta (1887). *Court and Private Life in the Time of Queen Charlotte, Vol I*. London: T Bentley & Son, p.265.

3. Llanover, Lady (1862). *The Autobiography and Correspondence of Mary Granville, Mrs Delaney, Vol III*. London, Richard Bentley, p.319.

4. Yorke, Philip (ed) (1898). *Letters of Princess Elizabeth of England*. London: T Fisher Unwin, pp.26-27.

5. Woolsey, Sarah Chauncey (1910). *The Diary and Letters of Frances Burney, Madame D'Arblay, Vol II*. Boston: Little, Brown, and Company, p.256.

6. Childe-Pemberton, William (1910). *The Romance of Princess Amelia*. London: G Bell & Sons Ltd, p.26.

7. *Morning Herald* (London, England), Monday, 9 March 1789; Issue 2615.

8. *Morning Post and Daily Advertiser* (London, England), Friday, 20 March 1789; Issue 4985.

9. *General Evening Post* (London, England), 11 March 1790 – 13 March 1790; Issue 8799.

10. *Morning Herald* (London, England), Thursday, 1 January 1789; Issue 2558.

11. *Morning Chronicle and London Advertiser* (London, England), Tuesday, 3 June 1788; Issue 5949.

12. *Public Advertiser* (London, England), Monday, 9 June 1788; Issue 16814.

13. Oulton, Walley Chamberlain (1819). *Authentic and Impartial Memoirs of Her Late Majesty, Charlotte, Queen of Great Britain and Ireland*. London: J Robins and Co, p.356.

14. Roberts, Jane (1910). *Royal Landscape: The Gardens and Parks of Windsor*. New Haven: Yale University Press, p.228.

15. Yorke, Philip (ed) (1898). *Letters of Princess Elizabeth of England*. London: T Fisher Unwin, p.34.

16. Aspinall, Arthur (1971). *The Correspondence of George, Prince of Wales, Volume VI*. Oxford: Oxford University Press, p.2515.

17. Iremonger, Lucille (1958). *Love and the Princesses*. New York: Thomas Y Crowell Company, p.146.

18. Glenbervie, Sylvester Douglas (1928). *The Diaries of Sylvester Douglas, Lord Glenbervie*. London: Constable & Co Ltd, p364.

19. Iremonger, Lucille (1958). *Love and the Princesses*. New York: Thomas Y Crowell Company, p.149.

20. *Morning Post* (London, England), Thursday, 5 February 1818; Issue 14679.

21. *Morning Post* (London, England), Wednesday, 8 April 1818; Issue 14732.

22. Yorke, Philip (ed) (1898). *Letters of Princess Elizabeth of England*. London: T Fisher Unwin, p.89.

23. *The Standard* (London, England), Thursday, 16 January 1840; Issue 4860.

Princess Mary, Duchess of Gloucester and Edinburgh (25 April 1776 – 30 April 1857)

1. Georgian Papers Online (http://gpp.rct.uk, March 2019) GEO/MAIN/36545-36546 Letter from Queen Charlotte to George III, 7 April 1805.
2. Taylor, Ernest (ed.) (1913). *The Taylor Papers*. London: Longmans, Green, and Co, pp.78-9.
3. Ibid., p.80.
4. *The Morning Post* (London, England), Monday, 3 June 1816; Issue 14156.
5. Müller, F Max (ed.) (1873). *Memoirs of Baron Stockmar, Vol I*. London: Longmans, Green, and Co, p.52.
6. Fitzgerald, Percy (1882). *The Royal Dukes and Princesses of the Family of George III, Vol II*. London: Tinsley Brothers, p.317.
7. Ibid., p.318.
8. *The Morning Chronicle* (London, England), Tuesday, 23 July 1816; Issue 14734.
9. *The Morning Post* (London, England), Tuesday, 16 July 1816; Issue 14193.
10. Bury, Charlotte Campbell, (1839). *Diary Illustrative of the Times of George the Fourth, Vol III*. London: Henry Colburn, pp.388-389.
11. *The Morning Post* (London, England), Tuesday, 2 December 1834; Issue 19964.
12. *Morning Post* (London, England), Wednesday, 19 November 1851; Issue 24318.
13. *Daily News* (London, England), Friday, 1 May 1857; Issue 3419.

Princess Sophia of the United Kingdom (3 November 1777 – 27 May 1848)

1. Woolsey, Sarah Chauncey (1910). *The Diary and Letters of Frances Burney, Madame D'Arblay, Vol I*. Boston: Little, Brown, and Company, pp.310-311.
2. Woolsey, Sarah Chauncey (1910). *The Diary and Letters of Frances Burney, Madame D'Arblay, Vol II*. Boston: Little, Brown, and Company, pp.310-311.
3. *Sun* (London, England), Wednesday, 2 October 1799; Issue 2193.
4. Aspinall, Arthur (ed.) (1963). *The Correspondence of George, Prince of Wales: Vol II*. London: Cassell, p.465.
5. Glenbervie, Sylvester Douglas (1928). *The Diaries of Sylvester Douglas, Lord Glenbervie*. London: Constable & Co Ltd, p.95.
6. Ibid., p.364.
7. Ibid., p.96.
8. Ibid., p.95.
9. Woolsey, Sarah Chauncey (1910). *The Diary and Letters of Frances Burney, Madame D'Arblay, Vol II.*Boston: Little, Brown, and Company, p.375.
10. Gillett, Eric (Walkey) (ed.) (1945). *Elizabeth Ham, by Herself.* London: Faber & Faber Ltd, p.48.

11. Childe-Pemberton, William (1910). *The Romance of Princess Amelia*. London: G Bell & Sons Ltd, pp.281-282.

12. Longford, Elizabeth (1989). *The Oxford Book of Royal Anecdotes*. Oxford: Oxford University Press, p.327.

13. Aspinall, A (ed.) (1949). *Letters of the Princess Charlotte, 1811-1817*. London: Home and Van Thal, p.99.

14. Ibid., p.88.

15. *The Morning Chronicle* (London, England), Thursday, 16 March 1820; Issue 15875.

16. *The Morning Post* (London, England), Tuesday 17 March, 1829; Issue 18177.

17. Tommy Garth died in 1873. His daughter, Georgiana, continued to pursue the royal family for money and recognition until her death in 1912.

18. Montgomery-Campbell, M (ed.) (1908). *Records of Stirring Times*. London: William Heinemann, p.87.

19. *The Morning Chronicle* (London, England), Monday, 29 May 1848; Issue 24524.

Princess Amelia of the United Kingdom
(7 August 1783 – 2 November 1810)

1. Burney, Frances (1854). *Diary and Letters of Madame D'Arblay, Vol VI*. London: Henry Colburn, p.179.

2. Ibid., p.181.

3. Childe-Pemberton, William (1910). *The Romance of Princess Amelia*. London: G Bell & Sons Ltd, p.39.

4. Ibid., pp.72-74.

5. Harcourt, Leveson Vernon (ed.) (1860). *The Diaries and Correspondence of the Right Hon. George Rose, Vol II*. London: Richard Bentley, pp.193-194.

6. Childe-Pemberton, William (1910). *The Romance of Princess Amelia*. London: G Bell & Sons Ltd, p.126.

7. Aspinall A (ed.) (1970). *Later Correspondence of George III: Vol V*. Cambridge: Cambridge University Press, p.355.

8. *Hampshire Telegraph and Sussex Chronicle etc* (Portsmouth, England), Monday, 5 November 1810; Issue 578.

9. *The Morning Post* (London, England), Monday, 5 November 1810; Issue 12406.

Afterword

1. Aspinall, Arthur (1962). *The Later Correspondence of George III, Vol II*. Cambridge: Cambridge University Press, p.3.

Index

Index

Index